# ON THE OTHER SIDE

A Palliative Care Nurse's Experience of Life with Cancer

Nurse Julia

Chemo Julia

Written By

**JULIA GARTSIDE-BENTLEY**

NEW ACTIVITY
PUBLICATIONS



Published by New Activity Publications
(a not-for-profit publisher)

ISBN 978-1-904969-69-3

# Dedication

To my wonderful mother who inspired me to be the nurse I became.

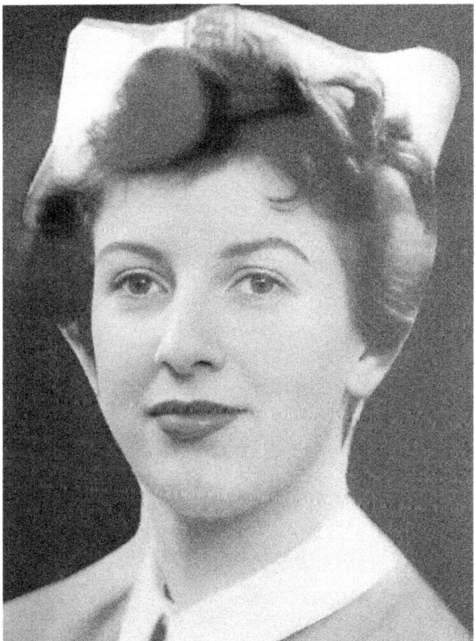

Staff Nurse Jean Catherine Murphy c. 1955

# Table of Contents

# Preface

When you embark on a journey with cancer, life will inevitably never be quite the same again. In a flash, you have been initiated into a life of what feels like endless consultations, blood tests, enforced change and relentless uncertainty. A time when, before you realise it, a total stranger soon comes to know more about your body than you do yourself.

My intention in writing about my experience with cancer has been to support others in trying to understand the impact a cancer diagnosis can have on people's lives, and how to positively contribute to both the potential and actual day-to-day challenges they may face. There will never be a standard format to a cancer journey, so I can only speak from my own personal experience and would never wish to be the voice of anyone else.

In January 2020, I can most definitely say my life changed forever. I was a happy and content wife and very proud mum, with our only son recently married to his high school sweetheart. I had a dream job, a fantastic network of family and friends, and my health – or so I thought.

As I started my shift as Nurse in Charge of the night shift at our local hospice, little did I know this was going to be the last shift I would ever work as a practicing, hands-on nurse. In what felt like the blink of an eye, all my hopes and dreams seemed to abruptly vanish, whisked away by three words: 'You have cancer'. I had suddenly morphed from a palliative care nurse, with over 37 years of general nursing experience, into one of my patients: a patient with Stage 4 ovarian cancer. I was embarking on a very personal and enlightening journey of my own, experiencing how it feels to be 'on the other side'. This wasn't how I had planned to see out my nursing days.

Some were saying it was inconceivable to them how a nurse, who has cared so much for others all their life, could end up having cancer themselves. The reply to them is simple: 'But why not?' No one is exempt from cancer, not even nurses!

Every so often, life will throw any one of us a curveball or two, which will inevitably force us to dig deep and try to manage something that may prove difficult, unexpected, personally challenging, or possibly all three; the dilemma we are left with is how we manage the strikes. With our lives totally unique and our exposure to basic life skills so varied, we will develop problem-solving strategies that will inevitably be different for us all.

Being quite a reflective and spiritual person, which I attribute to my life as a nurse, I utilised these traits to help me relinquish some of the exhausting and emotional burden I was carrying at the time and began to put my journey down on paper in the form of a diary. It really did prove to be such a cathartic and healing filler of unwelcome times, allowing me to express my thoughts, emotions and pain through the means of writing.

Then, as if cancer wasn't enough to try and get my head around, life then threw that second curveball which hit just as hard, and before I'd even had a chance to get up from the first one! However, this second challenge was to be a 'life-changing group challenge', you could say. It was like nothing most of us had ever seen in our lifetimes and with its relentless and ruthless uncertainty, the global Coronavirus pandemic callously, and with such momentum, took hold. It was an inconceivably painful and challenging time for every single person across the world and its devastation will undoubtedly remain with us forever.

Due to the subsequent enforced restrictions in place at the time, a considerable amount of my ongoing initial care was conducted away from the much needed and reassuring presence of my family and friends. We had no choice; no one had a choice, cancer or no cancer, dying or not. Anyone going into hospital had to go it alone and that was that! Our fellow patients and the staff became our invaluable stand-in families and friends, whilst our loved ones could only sit and wait at home. The comradery was so humbling as we all faced our worrying journeys and days together.

I chose to conclude my diary having been told, for the first time since that fateful day, that I was in remission. The words that followed have echoed through every day, from that moment to this, 'Now I want you to go and live your life to the full as I cannot promise you anything'. The chains were off, and I was once again free to try and get on with my life. Having target therapy every month until the following June was a relative doddle and minor inconvenience in comparison.

Living in my specific 'cancer bubble', my diary was purely a personal coping strategy and as such, I saw it as a tool to support that inner vulnerability I was carrying. Once I had stopped writing, it wasn't long before I was asked by colleagues, close family and friends to share my diary with them. When I look back, it felt like a request to try and fully understand the journey I had personally travelled and how they could possibly use this insight as a learning experience. And for me, I really wanted them to understand.

It was their responses that encouraged me to consider that my diary could possibly help someone else. Everyone was telling me how enlightening it was and that I needed to share my story to a much wider audience. My question was, 'But share it with who'? Unsure of who it could benefit, or if my story needed to be heard, I simply parked it in the drawer and focused on 'living my life'. On reflection, I'm quite glad I listened, as the following stages of my journey to date have been full of new and unique challenges for me. I have learnt so much about myself and how my life-changing experience has affected not only me, but so many others.

As a health professional myself, I could appreciate how, despite the structured training we all undertake in our individual fields of practice, every person's career pathway will encompass unique practical and often emotive experiences. It is through the exposure to real-life situations that we, and our patients, inevitably reap the rewards of that newfound knowledge, experience and confidence. Unquestionably, the individual patient will always remain the only person able to truly appreciate the day-to-day challenges of their cancer journey. So I hope, in sharing my experience, that others will be able to benefit from a clearer understanding and insight into living with cancer, irrespective of whether they are the supporter or the supported.

For me, I wasn't prepared to just sit and ride the storm – I still had a life to live. Whilst my experience has changed my life, it also brought me something new, a raw and holistic insight into a typical cancer journey, a new knowledge that has inadvertently gone on to help so many other people. So, if my book can help just one more person, albeit a fellow patient, relative, health professional, trainee nurse or doctor, then my journey has not been in vain.

# Chapter 1

# Living the Dream

My life has been nurtured by wonderful parents, who wanted nothing more than for me to be happy, build my dreams and live them out as best I can. Coming from a family with a variety of medical and nursing backgrounds, I think nursing was probably in my blood from day one.

Whilst never pushed into nursing, my aspirations were clearly fostered from this heritage, with the biggest contribution undoubtedly coming from my wonderful, now late mother. Determined and focused on becoming as good a nurse as she was, I set off on a path that I hoped would enable me to fulfil one of my biggest dreams in life.

After qualifying as a nurse in 1985, the learning really started. Heading out onto the wards was a daunting experience for all of us. There's nothing like standing out in a crowd, advertising your hard-earned knowledge with your pristine white uniform, Petersham belt and shiny new buckle, along with your beautifully folded nurse's cap, hoping to come across as another reassuring, confident presence that every patient could rely on, rather than the 'rookie' who would likely be practising on them at some point in their stay.

You convince yourself you still don't know enough to be a qualified nurse, with everyone undoubtedly expecting you to know everything. You're taught in your training never to let the patient see what you are really thinking, when deep down all you wanted to do was run in the opposite direction or hide in the sluice all day, happily cleaning everything down with tiny alcohol wipes if needs be.

I recall qualifying as a State Enrolled Nurse (SEN) back in 1985 at Shrewsbury Hospital in Shropshire, a time when the foundations were laid in supporting my life as a nurse. I was like a little sponge, soaking up every bit of knowledge and embracing every opportunity to see and learn something new.

I was constantly facing new challenges and wanting to showcase my passion to make a difference, whatever shape or form that took. Sometimes, that meant taking myself out of my comfort zone for just a moment to 'dip my toe in the water', and other times it was my seniors giving me a hefty nudge into the deep end.

It wasn't long before I moved to Stafford, finding myself working in trauma and cold surgery orthopaedics. It was a busy ward with little respite, but there was so much for me to learn. Nursing was changing quickly, and I felt if I didn't bite the bullet and do some additional training, my knowledge and skills as an SEN would soon lose any recognition. The training created new opportunities and experiences, equipping me with an enriched knowledge that would support new roles and responsibilities. With that additional training under my belt, I was soon a Registered Nurse, a 'bluey'.

I can't believe how quickly time passed. I was on Orthopaedics for over 18 years and in that time, I married, gave birth to our first-born child and moved house twice. I was able to create the perfect work-life balance which was so important to me. My standards were high, I was always driven to be a great role model and through my mentoring of trainee nurses, I would love to share my knowledge, skills and wisdom, never forgetting an element of appropriately placed humour for good measure.

I always seemed to be that nurse who walked towards a challenge, with colleagues telling me, 'You're always so good with things like this'. I'm certainly not blowing my own trumpet, but it never felt uncomfortable having to face difficult situations or just being there to listen. It was simply something that felt so natural. Nurses are not built from a standard mould; we are individuals with very personal passions, interests and career goals and where one person may excel in a specific field of practice, others may struggle.

I can recall my mother telling me that we can often be making a difference without realising it in ourselves. It might be a simple acknowledgement of someone's presence or vulnerability, or perhaps a passing smile or touch. She told me, 'You are never going to change everyone's day, but if doing what you do can change just one person's day, then that was your reason for getting out of bed that day'. Wise words that I've shared with so many colleagues and student nurses throughout my career, and I hope that by doing so I have contributed positively to the lives of so many hard-working nurses when times have been tough, or when they simply needed to stop for a moment and reflect.

After 18 years of working in Trauma Orthopaedics, my focus had started to switch to a new challenge, somewhere that I would be able to utilise my years of nursing experience and knowledge whilst still helping others, but this time it would mean working in a completely different field of practice. I wanted to be a palliative care nurse, an often-challenging speciality for anyone, a place where the care offers relief, but not cure. My mother used to tell me that I would make a fantastic palliative care nurse, I just needed to choose the right time to explore this as apparently, many nurses in this field are known to hit 'burnout'.

With an additional year of personal and self-funded study, I felt ready and prepared to apply. I was over the moon when that call came through: I had been successful at interview and the job was mine. It was so hard to leave my trusted work family/friends behind as I prepared to embark on my 'new adventure'. I won't deny, the emotional turmoil was a very challenging hurdle, but the decision to take that leap of faith had been made and nothing was going to hold me back.

I can wholeheartedly say that it felt as if my ability and desire to care for others had been set free once again. The last couple of years of working in the hospital were so hard. We were more frequently being denied essential resources, the tools needed to ensure a safe place to those entrusted into our care. We were all too frequently facing unwelcome and unethical dilemmas which would put all our hard-earned study at risk, potentially compromising our ability to continue practicing. This had become the norm for so many other nurses in practice. It was soul-destroying.

I frequently experienced the expectation to run a 32-bed Trauma Orthopaedic unit overnight, with only myself and an auxiliary to deliver and prioritise patients' care: the post-surgery, emergency admissions, dependent patients, infusions, blood transfusions, medications, personal care, the confused, nursing records. It was inevitable that the so desperately-needed emotional support found itself nudged down the priority list. Hence, it was often 03:00 before I could get to someone who was lying awake and needing to talk. It was, quite honestly, any nurse's worst nightmare. Believe me when I say that I didn't take it lying down! The only words I can think of to describe that particular time for me are *disheartening*, *demoralising*, *crippling*, *stressful*, *unsafe*, *unethical*, *demotivating* and *unrecognisable*.

It was January 2003 and I was back living the dream, giving my usual 110% to each and every patient that I had the privilege to care for. I once again had the time, resources and support I needed to ensure the very best of care was given to everyone, to the best of my ability. It was so rewarding and also alien to be able to give my time and support to every visitor that came into the building. It's so obvious to me now, but you can't expect to deliver holistic care without caring for the very people who play such an important part in someone's life. Whether it be a relative, friend, neighbour or colleague, each person is as important as the next. It wasn't unusual for some handovers to take longer to discuss the visitor's needs than those of the patient's.

Over the next 17 years I built a new work family, more calm, professional, funny, likeminded people, each with the same desire to ultimately help those in need and make a difference. They would offer their knowledge, experience, professional and personal skills, always happy to go that extra mile in order to support each person's unique journey. I will always remember my induction day, when we were told, ‘Patients don’t come here to die, they come to live, and we support them in living as best a life as we possibly can’. It's so true; whilst we cannot cure our patients of their illnesses, we can support them to live through the often rollercoaster trajectory of their illness.

Hospices offer their services to people with progressive life-limiting conditions at various points along this rollercoaster ride, and whilst many of our patients do have cancer, our services are not exclusive to cancer patients. The reasons for an admission can range from a couple of days’ respite to a period of assessment, control of various symptoms, psychological support and also end of life care. Some may not even require admission, instead being directed to one of the many additional services hospices can offer.

It is so incredibly rewarding and humbling to be able to help someone through their darkest of times. Regardless of professional understanding or mutual experience, you can only imagine what each person’s journey must have entailed, never undermining its rippling effect on those around them. Nobody can or will fully understand another person’s unique experience, and even when they have walked in very similar shoes, those shoes weren't their shoes.

# Chapter 2

# The Other Side

Four months ago, we celebrated one of the best days ever, when our only son Ross married his high school sweetheart. It was a perfect day in every way, and I don't mind saying that I felt amazing and was more than happy to soak up every single compliment that came my way. Followed by a fantastic joint family holiday, along with the newly-weds, in Turkey, I look back and feel so grateful that we had such a wonderful time, building treasured memories whilst totally oblivious to what lay ahead for us all.

**Ross & Nic's wedding & 'Family Honeymoon' August 2019**

With the 'joys' of the menopause embedded in my everyday life, I was used to my body and head not feeling or behaving like they should. So, when do you decide that this is different than usual? Generally, none of us want to come across as hypochondriacs, so perhaps we convince ourselves that we probably don't need to make that doctor's appointment, as it's probably 'just' hormones or middle-age spread anyway. Maybe it's the thought of having to talk about your 'private parts', periods, or your sex life, let alone having to undergo an intimate examination and worrying about how embarrassed or uncomfortable you will feel.

For some women, whether because of their ethnic, religious or cultural backgrounds or maybe historic life traumas or otherwise, the need to conduct an intimate procedure, or even to be close to a doctor, may be particularly difficult and stressful. This can often be enough to put some women off visiting the doctor with new or existing health concerns. It's been identified through certain research that women feel that there's a stigma associated with gynaecological cancers, citing the assumption of sexual promiscuity as one of the contributing factors.

Whatever the reason, it is never going to be worth compromising your life over; nothing is ever worth that price. It's incredibly sad to read how millions of people with varying symptoms have been recorded as having delayed doctor's appointments purely because of embarrassment. This has been reflected in numerous articles over recent years stressing how, sadly, too many people are 'literally dying of embarrassment'. Ongoing research continues to highlight gynaecological cancer as the cancer type most likely to be affected by less timely diagnosis, and delays in diagnosis and early treatment frequently result in poorer cancer outcomes.

For most people there will be a reassuring chat with the doctor, perhaps a blood test and possibly a routine scan, with a follow-up appointment to confirm that everything comes back clear. Be assured that at no point was your visit to the doctor ever a wasted journey.

Commonly, nurses and doctors are notorious for self-diagnosing and avoiding visits to the doctor where at all possible. They often believe they should know if the symptoms are something or nothing, and don't want to appear stupid or be seen as overreacting. They preach to others, but many foolishly fail to heed their own advice.

It was January 20th, 2020, and I had started to become increasingly aware of some abdominal bloating, along with a pressure-type discomfort when I sat down. The best way I could describe it was as if I was sitting down with something the size of a cricket ball inside of me. Constipation has been a problem for many years, especially with working shifts and an underactive thyroid, but I was now feeling like I was not fully emptying my bowel when I went to the toilet, and that was something new. Since being perimenopausal, I'd had to have several scans and been told I had a fibroid so typically, trying to self-diagnose, I thought maybe it could be that, or possibly a uterine prolapse? Either way, it didn't feel right, and I was telling myself that if I need an operation, I need an operation. Surprisingly, despite my clinical knowledge and background in nursing, I never actually thought at this point that it might be cancer.

Having just finished my night shift, I was more than ready for my bed and completely oblivious to the fact that I had just worked my last ever shift as a Senior Staff Nurse on the Inpatient Unit at our local hospice. It's 08:40 and I'm sat quietly in the doctor's waiting area as Sue calls me in, and we have our usual little catchup with each other before I start to explain my symptoms. Typical nurse, I'm reading her body language for clues as to her level of concern. She examines me and whilst trying to reassure me, she admits she's unsure of what's going on. I can see she is concerned as she explains the tests she is going to organise urgently. She includes a Ca 125, which I'm aware is a cancer marker blood test used to look for signs of ovarian cancer. My heart is racing a bit, but I'm glad tests are going to be done. I really hope it's something reversible.

I hadn't said anything to Andy up until this point as I didn't want to worry him unnecessarily, but I'm now thinking I really need to say something. Automatically, he asks loads of questions and wants me to assure him that there is nothing to worry about and that I'm not worried, but I can't.

I'm thinking I might have just gone from being a nurse to a patient in a day.

It's been 48 hours, pretty much to the dot, when the phone rings and it's the doctors to say Sue had asked if I can go to the surgery to discuss the blood results. My heart rate has just gone up several notches, I can feel my pulse pounding in my neck and chest, especially as it's a Saturday morning and appointments are usually so difficult to get on a weekend. Andy is clearly worried and asking me what I think, searching for my reassurance. Whilst inside I'm really hoping it's good news, I just know that it's not going to be the case. Either way, I can't give him the answer he wants, and I know he knows that really.

I don't remember much about the journey, but we arrive at the surgery and it's so quiet, being a Saturday. We don't even get as far as sitting down when Sue's consulting room door opens, and she calls us through. She's already placed two chairs for us as she closes the door. Her face says it all. 'I'm so sorry chick, but it's not good news.'

She gives me a minute to process what she's just said before she continues. 'I'm afraid you have ovarian cancer, your cancer markers (Ca

125) are raised and some of your other bloods are typically raised too'. With knowing very little about cancer markers, I ask what they are. 'They're 4274.' I asked if that's high and she confirmed it was. They were raised and not just a bit, but massively. Apparently, the normal range is usually anything up to 35. The bottom has just fallen out of my world. This was not in my plans for the future!

Believe me, there are times when you really wish you weren't a nurse – and a palliative care one at that. Too much knowledge is not always helpful in these moments. Turning to look at Andy, he's clearly convinced she's just given me a life sentence, as he breaks down in total disbelief at what we're hearing. I am completely numb, the only thing I can feel being my tears as they start to slowly run down my face. Sue looks completely devastated and I can't help but feel so sorry for her, having to break this news to us. So I randomly apologise to her. She smiles at what she calls 'my typical concern for others' and explains she had been rung last night by her colleague Dave, who we also know well, telling her the results. She had apparently been awake all night worrying about having to break the news to me and whether she should leave it until after the weekend or call me in today. As difficult as it's been to hear, I'm glad she didn't wait.

I tell her about my wonderful Aunty Pam who had also been recently diagnosed with ovarian cancer. I explain we were very close and how I think the world of her. Her diagnosis hit me very hard at the end of last year and now I have to tell her I am about to embark on the same journey. She's already very fragile and this is going to be so difficult to break to her. Sue listens with her unquestionable empathy, assuring me we would fight this together and that she was always there for me. 'You have my number, don't you chick? So, if there's anything, any time, you know where I am.'

Andy and I sit in the car for what seems like ages, no words, just completely broken. Time has come to a silent and complete standstill. We acknowledge we need to tell Ross first and foremost, but I'm really struggling to accept what I'm about to do. This is the last thing anyone would want to be doing and I can't believe I am having to do it, especially as his mother, who loves him dearly, and the last thing I want to do is risk breaking his heart too. We relay the news as gently but as honestly as possible, and whilst he tries to remain composed it's evident he's clearly gutted as he tries to absorb what I'm saying. He's so like me in many ways, as he tries to suppress his emotions for now and focus on the practicalities of what needs to happen next. I love how calm, reassuring and mature he is, but at the end of the day, he's still my 'little boy' who I'm always going to worry about and right now, causing him this pain and worry is so difficult to accept.

I wonder how my parents would have dealt with me being poorly. I can only imagine how any parent would feel, regardless of age, hearing such news, and I know that whilst both my mother and father would have been absolutely devastated, they would unquestionably have been by my side to support us every step of the way.

This is all so surreal. I have witnessed devastating news being given on many occasions and provided my support in various guises, but I have never been able to fully appreciate the complex chain reaction of processes and emotions that can follow, until now. How different my perception was, even as a nurse, before cancer.

So, as I move on to the rest of the family, I can feel the shellshock rippling from them as their lives too are turned upside down. The reactions range from initial silence, tears, disbelief, well-meant platitudes and then anger. The questions start and the main one is, 'How can you go from being so well to being told this?' Inwardly I'm thinking, 'I know, but I have and I don't really know what you want me to say'. It's a perfectly natural response, but one that has no answers. While everyone is reacting, Andy keeps looking at me, still in his state of shock, sitting close as we all try to process my bombshell and what lies ahead of me.

I don't think I can sit through any more exhausting reactions and well-meant platitudes. We need to leave and let everyone process what has just happened in their own ways. Leaving a wake of total devastation behind us, we still need to face our closest friends and again watch and listen as the shellshock hits. Totally drained, I don't think I can take anymore, I'm grieving for my happy life, and really need to get home and it just be the two of us.

Within days I'm at the first scan appointment, an ultrasound scan. I understand the standard two-week NHS Cancer Pathway, but it's so scary to be called in so quickly. I appreciate that the sonographer cannot say much about what she has seen, if anything, and she assures me she will email the results to the doctor today. By midafternoon, Sue is ringing me to say she has the results and did we both want to come to the surgery to discuss them? It's all moving so incredibly quickly and while this should be so reassuring, I'm petrified, we're both petrified – but we need to know what we're facing.

Well, it's most definitely there. I apparently have 'a large complex mass' about the size of a clenched fist, along with a buildup of ascites (accumulation of fluid between the lining of the abdomen and my abdominal organs). Everything has gone from my head and all I can think of is what's been happening to my body. Unquestionably, I'm feeling so much emotional pain, but I don't seem to have any tears onboard right now. I'm just stunned at how something can grow to this size and me not know about it until it's caused such harm. I guess this is how this type of cancer gets its name: the silent killer. Thoughts bounce around in my head, 'Are we in time, or are we too late?' I'm not going to get those questions answered anytime soon and as most people who know me will know, I don't do waiting too well.

Two days later and we're sat with one of the gynaecology consultants. I wanted Andy and Ross with me so that we could absorb and try to process the information together and give them the chance to ask their own questions. I have prompted them to ask anything or repeat anything they don't quite understand. It's so hard to retain every bit of information given to you at hospital appointments, so the more of us there, the better.

Clinical history out of the way, a physical examination was next. Really not a very pleasant examination on this occasion, as they needed to try and obtain a tissue sample and I can't deny that it was quite painful, but at least they were particularly mindful of my dignity and the discomfort I was in, offering genuine and very welcome reassurance. We now have to wait for my CT scan and relevant histology results. Everyone is very clear about the plan of care, which is what I wanted and needed. It's offering me a tiny, but welcome, bit of control over things.

Not long back home and I'm feeling totally exhausted with everything that is going on at the moment. Then the phone rings and it's the X-ray department to see if I'm able to go right now to get my CT scan done. Of course, I'm so tired, but at least that'll be another thing done that I won't have to wait for, so we go straight there and get called through straight away. I change into my 'designer gowns', with the standard advice, 'the first one with the opening at the back and the second one opening at the front', which prevents you from flashing your behind at everyone as you stroll through the department.

I get called into a treatment room where they soon cannulate me, and from there it's not long before I'm called into the scanner room. Dressed only in my 'designer gowns' and having been encouraged to leave my ankle boots on, I can't tell you how 'special' I feel as I walk past Andy, who is probably thinking, 'What a stunner' – NOT.

For those of you out there who have been fortunate enough not to require a CT scan, the tunnel isn't as frightening and claustrophobic as its size projects, or as people might 'kindly' choose to tell you. I'm asked to lie down and place my arms above my head. As the radiographer connects me to an infusion pump, she explains that she will remotely inject a contrast dye into my cannula which will make me feel like I'm having a hot flush and cause a sensation as if I have wet myself, but reassures me that I won't have done. All I can focus on now is that I don't wet myself! The procedure only takes a few minutes and I'm incredibly relieved to know I'm dry. With my cannula soon removed, I can get changed again. We must wait a short while to ensure I don't have any adverse effects from the dye, then I'm off home again.

It's been an emotionally charged week for us both and we're shattered. We sit and reflect on just where that week has gone. We can't fault the NHS at all; they are moving so quickly with everything and treating me with such dignity and compassion. I can safely say that it feels like the NHS certainly know my body far better than I do right now!

I'm mindful that my swollen tummy is getting worryingly bigger and increasingly uncomfortable by the day. I look about 8 months pregnant, but without the anticipated joy. It's the ascites they have seen on the ultrasound scan starting to build up in volume, which is not unusual, but my nurse's head is telling me that this is developing quickly and I hadn't expected it to happen quite so fast – another enlightening moment that highlighted a much clearer understanding of ascites and how they can impact a person's day-to-day life.

Friends from work are messaging me daily. I've suddenly gone off sick and no one knows why. Their concern is so lovely. We are a close-knit team and clearly, they want me to know they are thinking of me.... with 'whatever's the matter'. I'm not ready to say anything just yet, I'm still processing what we've been told, and we still have more information to come. I'm not liking just saying 'Thanks' and 'I'm OK', but I really want to stick with this for now. Andy, Ross and I need to know everything and have the plan clear in our heads before we share this with them, as their hospice heads will very quickly be thinking all sorts, and I don't want the potential fallout from that until I can get to tell them exactly what we know ourselves. I hope they will understand my hesitance.

# Chapter 3

# Vulnerability at its Best

My lovely friend and ex-colleague Clair, who has turned out to be my Oncology Clinical Nurse Specialist (CNS), has been so supportive, insisting I call or message her anytime. Over the weekend I mentioned about my ascites and how they have increased considerably. It's unbelievable to see how quickly I have changed and that's petrified me, especially when I can't get all those lovely ladies I've care for over the years, with their huge tummies, out of my mind. She's reassured me that she's going to liaise with the gynae CNSs today and ask them to contact me, which they do. Linsey, my gynae CNS, reassures me that she is going to request an urgent paracentesis (a drainage of the fluid from my abdomen) for as soon as possible this week and will advise me as soon as she's been able to arrange it.

In less than 24 hours my discomfort has reached an unbearable crescendo and nothing has helped. Struggling to eat, with a tiny, almost nonexistent appetite and drinking, but barely passing any urine, I tire so easily as my breathing is also becoming more and more difficult. The nights are so long, as I can't seem to get comfortable, only being able to sleep on my back and propped up with 2–3 pillows. Andy is wakeful with the slightest movement from me, followed with, 'Are you OK?'

Walking upstairs is now such an unwelcome challenge as I'm having to hold the banister firmly to pull myself up, slowly conquering one step at a time, and when I reach the top I can't move until I get my breath again. I feel like a 90-year-old pregnant woman in her final trimester!! I'm so relieved that we had the downstairs toilet put in as I'm now, slowly and cautiously, only coming down once a day in the morning and then only going up again when I'm ready for bed. Without the downstairs toilet I would have had to restrict myself to living upstairs.

Unable to take much more, I give Linsey another call. She advises me to present to A&E where they will admit me. Without hesitation we are on our way, seat reclined and barely a word from me, as I just stare ahead. There's a song on the radio I've heard three times already today and it's starting to annoy me now, I don't know why; it's not even the lyrics.

We arrive and I'm soon booked in and it's not long before I'm taken through into a side room. It's not the most welcoming of spaces, with a lonely patient's trolley in the centre of the room, a chair, no window and the door shut too, but I really don't care. There's a purple bow on the wall of my room and I really hope it's been carelessly left from a previous patient. Already feeling so incredibly ill and emotional, I'm trying so hard not to cry, as I ask Andy to please take it down and put it face down on the shelf. He looks at me, totally bemused, and with the emotion I'm feeling right now, I don't really want to have to explain that this is a sign the staff use to let them know that the person in this room is palliative and coming to the end of their life. He reads my vulnerability and doesn't push me on it, simply putting it on the shelf and asking, 'Is that better?" I just manage a quiet 'Thank you'.

The department is busy as we patiently wait our turn. Eventually my turn has arrived and after several doctors, a bit of 'poking and prodding', bloods, cannulas, drips and an X-ray, I'm finally being transferred to the Surgical Assessment Unit (SAU) and it's not long before Clair pops in to see me. The symptoms have really started to get to me now, having never felt so desperately ill or this vulnerable and frightened before.

I really don't think my body is going to take much more now, but I can't say anything as I don't want to frighten Andy more than he is right now. I have always been the coper in our relationship, and he would agree, but right now I'm really struggling and I don't want to let him see how frightened I really am. He is going to have to drive himself home shortly and then be there worrying on his own, so I just lie or sit quietly and say the odd word or two.

A lovely gynaecology consultant, Miss San, walks in and introduces herself to us both and so quickly, I feel reassured by her calm and gentle manner. Never having met before, she kneels beside me, gently takes my hand and listens with such natural compassion and genuine empathy. She explains everything to us and checks whether we need her to go over anything again. As she leaves, we both acknowledge this overwhelming sense of relief, believing I am safe, completely safe in her hands.

Despite the endless intravenous infusions, I still barely pass any urine, so it's suggested that I have a bladder scan to see what's happening. Unsurprisingly, having just been to the toilet and only managing to pass about 5 mls, they identify a residual urine of 999mls+ sitting in my bladder. I know what's coming next. Just before I give my consent to a catheter, my nurse's head questions the accuracy of the reading, given that I have a large tumour sitting in my abdomen. While this may be the case, I acknowledge that my output by no means reflects how much liquid I'm taking in, and how dangerous this could prove to be, so I agree to the catheter. The student nurse is keen to observe, and I'm asked if I consent to her assisting the staff nurse. Being a student mentor lead myself, I've always been keen for students to be given every opportunity to observe and learn, and to be honest I feel so poorly, I really don't care either way.

I've performed numerous catheterisations throughout my nursing career and all I can say is, when I got to experience the procedure for myself, what an enlightening experience it was! I wouldn't mind, but it didn't make a lot of difference to my comfort as I still ended up on hourly urine measurements, barely passing between 5-10mls an hour, but at least they were able to monitor me a lot more effectively.

After 48 hours of feeling so ill, and with the accumulation of sleep deprivation – having also witnessed and overheard some incredibly sad and distressing admissions through the nights – I'm moved to the gynaecology ward, where the ladies all seem really nice and give me a lovely, comforting welcome. My immediate neighbour to the right of me sits down awkwardly and explains she is two days post-op after a hysterectomy. The lady opposite me casually tells me she's having investigations relating to her cancer and to be fair, that didn't shock me, given my knowledge and experience of caring for very ill cancer patients and just seeing how extremely cachexic (extreme weight loss and muscle-wasting) she looked.

It's visiting time and Andy, Ross, Nic and one of my dearest 'besties', Pam, walk into the bay. It's so lovely to see them all, even though I still feel so ill. Ross and Nic have brought a gift bag full of goodies for me. My abdomen is so distended that I can't bend forward to lift it from the end of the bed and with the chair and table at the side of me, I ask Nic to kindly pass me the contents instead. Puzzle books, colouring pens/pencils, magazines, sweeties, chocolates... and then she passes me a parcel wrapped in tissue paper. I'm puzzled, as they all look at me with big grins. It turned out to be a pregnancy test. My reaction is a staged 'ha-ha, very funny', given I'd been saying I looked 9 months pregnant. Ross asks me to look again. It says 'pregnant' in the little window!!!!!!!!! Well, that's it, I can't hold back the tears. We are expecting our first grandchild, the next generation of Gartside-Bentleys. It's just the best news ever and a perfect focus for us all right now. They look so incredibly happy: that's all I've ever wanted for them.

The nurse has just been and told me I'm going down for my paracentesis in a couple of hours. So, they're going to insert a drain into my abdomen, allowing the fluid (ascites) to drain away. Surprisingly, especially for a nurse anyway, there is no fear, no apprehension, I'm just focused on being able to breathe again and feeling better. Looking back over my years of caring for people with significantly distended abdomens, I can't quite believe what all these people had actually been dealing with day to day, and how frightened and uncomfortable they must have felt. I actually feel quite ashamed that I hadn't previously understood and appreciated just what they were going through, alongside feeling so incredibly uncomfortable.

A lovely Health Care Assistant asked if I want a wash/shower before I went to have my drain in. I asked if she could possibly help me as I really didn't think I could manage without her help, and that realisation felt like it had broken me. I had become so vulnerable and dependent, needing someone else to look after my basic care needs, needs that I had always been in total control of since I was a child.

She did everything for me, and it was enough for me to just stand under the shower holding onto the hand rail as I let her wash me. She asked if I felt able to dry myself, but I really didn't feel I could. I had to sit down as I was about to collapse, feeling like I was slowly suffocating, with my diaphragm running out of capacity to move. As I sat, slumped in the shower chair, she dried me off and helped me to put my gown on. Her time and patience had been invaluable, with my simple 'Thank you' not really reflecting the impact of what she'd done for me. I can now truly appreciate first-hand the difference that the smallest of gestures of help can make to those in need.

Now in the Imaging room, I'm greeted by a doctor, two staff nurses and two HCAs. Whilst they are so lovely, I'm still starting to feel a little bit anxious as they open all the packs in readiness. With routine observations complete, the doctor scans me again, to locate the fluid and decide where best to insert the drain. Everything is done with well-rehearsed care and precision, while a lovely nurse takes my hand and I tell her my very recent news: I'm going to become a granny!! Everyone reacts and seems clearly delighted for me and just for a short while, I feel I'm so much more than 'the patient with ovarian cancer who needs a paracentesis'. I'm Julia, a living, breathing human being with emotions and a life story to tell; and these total strangers have just reminded me of all that, with a very natural, heartfelt sincerity.

The relief from the drain is very quick, as in about 30 minutes to an hour I have drained over 3 litres. I'm carefully monitored to ensure my blood pressure is coping with the amount of fluid loss over this time. Back on the ward, the poor nurses are at my bedside constantly to empty this rapidly filling drainage bag, as unfortunately, Imaging didn't have the larger drainage bags which would have made the nurses' lives so much easier. I'm constantly apologizing, as if they don't have enough to do.

Unable to have a shower whilst the drain is in, it looked like I was going to be having delightful strip washes for the time being. It's really not the most refreshing of experiences, but at least I could do this myself now and it was certainly better than nothing. In the bathroom I look at my naked reflection in the full-length mirror and ask myself, 'What on earth is happening to me?' I can't quite take all this in. I'd lost loads of weight from my face; my neck looks all 'scraggy' and my shrunken boobs look more like a couple of poached eggs stuck on my chest. My tummy is all distorted, with a bulky dressing and tube coming out of my side and catheter tubing dangling between my legs, as I place my urine bag on one chair and the drainage bag on the side of the sink. Tethered to my bags, I try to dress myself without knocking my two cannulas out from the back of my hand. I love to wear pyjamas at home, but I can't stand anything round my tummy right now, so I've had to ask another 'bestie', Shereen, to pick me up a few nightdresses. Albeit perfect, I put one on and feel like it's added another 15–20 years onto me. If I'm honest, I don't think I can entirely blame the nightie.

Over several days ahead, the flow does slow down and I've nearly reached a total of 12 litres' drainage. I am eating again and my appetite is beginning to return. The consultant wants to introduce me to the world of supplement drinks and tells me I must try and have three Ensure Compacts a day, treating them more as a prescription rather than an optional extra. The lady opposite advises me she always has the vanilla – 'It's the best one' – and definitely chilled. I give it a go and whilst I wouldn't crave them, they're actually not too bad.

Now moving independently, without feeling quite so breathless, I can say I'm starting to feel so much more comfortable in general. I'm able to walk out into the corridor and back without help now. I look 'wonderful,' with my dark green anti-embolus socks on and my drainage bag tucked into my dressing gown pocket. Friends and family continue to be welcome visitors in the afternoons. They're a helpful distraction from everything that's happening, as I try to move the conversation to anything other than my cancer.

My wonderful friend Lynn has been keeping her eye on me, albeit by text, as she lives in Shrewsbury. She too has gone through a cancer journey and has been an absolute rock to me. Every appointment, she texts me to say she 'will be right beside me and holding my hand tightly'. I'm gutted that she's had to experience cancer too, but I feel that in offering so openly to share her experience with me, as well as being a very special friend of 37 years, she definitely qualifies as one of my trusty rocks. She's such an amazing and inspirational woman.

It's been 3–4 days now and it's still draining around 250–500 mls daily. My consultant explains how it's a potential site for infection and now that things have slowed right down, it needs to come out and then we can look at going home. I'm a bit hesitant about the idea, as I really want it to stop draining altogether and never come back. I never again want to feel like I had in these recent days, but I understand that whilst the drain is there, it's also likely to drain still.

Well, I can't say the removal was nice because it really wasn't; in fact, it was bloody awful, despite being told to keep taking lots of deep breaths. The nurse tells me it's because it has been in for several days and then they do tend to be more difficult to remove. And I'm surprised I've not broken the poor assistant nurse's kindly-offered hand! Ah well, it's out now and everyone seems okay. I'm no longer attached to my 'designer bag' and 'looking forward' to two days of 'refreshing' strip washes ahead of me until the dressing can come off.

It's discharge day and I'm tentatively walking out of the hospital, thinking how lovely it feels to have the fresh air on my face; it's like medicine for the soul. However, the reality of just how weak and vulnerable I am still comes as an unwelcome wake-up call. Andy offers his arm to hold onto as I walk so slowly, telling him my legs feel like jelly. After being tied up in rush hour traffic for what seemed like ages, it was lovely to be home with my familiar comforts around me, a wonderful welcome from Trigger (our dog) and not forgetting a very comfy bed waiting for me upstairs.

Now settled on the settee with a nice snuggly blanket over my legs and a 'cuppa tea', Andy and I have a chance to have a good catch-up and talk about everything that's happening to us right now, as we learn to adjust to our new way of life. It was never possible to sit and talk properly in hospital and we've got a lot to talk over. I want to find out how he was really managing, especially when I've not been there with him. He does tend to hold things in as a rule, and finds talking about his raw emotions an uncomfortable exercise, but he needs to start – and start with me, the one who can read him like a book.

After a good chat, he recognises it would be good to pop and have a talk with one of our GPs, David, and spend some time addressing his feelings. Acknowledging and treating the psychological and emotional impact of such challenging journeys, for whoever may be affected, is vital. Mental health is essential for our ability as humans not only to think, but also to function, interact with one another, enjoy life and try and earn a living. Some will say, 'But it's not about me', and feel they are 'being selfish'. But this is never the case.

I've worked with David in the past and I know he is aware of our situation, as he was the doctor who rang Sue that evening with my initial blood results. Andy has been supported by David before and has a lot of respect and faith in him, as do I. I've made him an appointment for this Wednesday, something I can actually do for him for a change. I'm trying to remain his reliable steadying rock, but I know I just don't have the inner strength to address and talk through these very raw emotions, and to be fair, I think he would hold back anyway for fear of upsetting me. I'm quite sure that what he really needs to talk about and explore is probably not what I want or need to hear, at this moment in time anyway.

# Chapter 4

# The Plan

The past couple of days have offered us both some extremely welcome respite. When I say respite, I mean the little things that we all usually take for granted every day, that now feel so precious. On my first night home from hospital, I can't remember hitting the pillow. I think it was because I was able to snuggle onto my side again as I used to do, rather than propping myself up all night to ensure I could breathe.

Andy comes in, having left me to have a wonderful lie-in. For a change, I feel like a bit of breakfast. 'Matron Andy' tells me to stay put and off he goes to prepare my feast of one Weetabix and a cup of tea. He sits on the bed and tells me he has made me an appointment at our hairdressers so I can go and get my hair washed and blow-dried. With not being able to have a shower for 48 hours, this is such a lovely thought, especially when it's been well over a week since I was last able to wash it. Just to be able to sit there and let someone run warm running water over your head and gently massage it was wonderful. The guys are all so good to me. They're already aware I'm not well and as such, take great care of me and reassure me that I can pop in anytime and just have my hair washed and blow-dried, point blank refusing to let me pay.

That's not all. I've also got a nail appointment this afternoon. Nic had told me that when her relative was going through chemotherapy, they were advised to have their nails painted a dark colour to help protect them through the chemo. I'd never heard of this before, but with this in my mind and now being off sick, for what I imagine will be a very long time, I ask for just that. Being a nurse, it's quite alien for me to even have my nails painted, but in fact they look pretty cool.

I'm finally allowed to take my dressing off tonight, so I can have my first shower in what feels like ages. My tummy is still swollen, but not quite as much as before. I have bruising where my drain was and also where the biopsy was taken, and my skin is a bit angry from where the dressings had been, but it will settle. After sitting on the bed so he could listen out for me in the shower, Andy comes in and asks, 'How's that feel?' With a smile on my face, all I can say is, 'It feels incredible, I actually feel almost human again'. Such a basic daily function that most of us are fortunate enough to generally think nothing of – that is, until you're denied it.

Yesterday, with my hair, nails and shower, meant so much. I was able to feel a bit more like myself again and it was so reassuring. But I'm not sure and I really don't want to consider this, but I think the fluid is starting to come back already, and it's only been two days since I left hospital. Once again, my urine output is tailing off, my waistline is disappearing and I'm feeling tired with doing very little. I'm nowhere near as bad as I was last time, but I'm so upset at how quickly it's returned, and worried at the thought of it escalating to another crisis point. The nights are once again unforgiving for us both, and as we find ourselves watching the night sky turn to day, I ask myself, 'Is this how life is going to be?' and, 'Will I ever have the chance to enjoy life again?'

With my tiny appetite I can see I'm starting to lose more weight (muscle tone) and when I look in the mirror, my clothes are really loose – well, everywhere but around my tummy. I pull on the support of Clair and Linsey again, who reassure me that they will liaise with the relevant people and have a contingency plan in place.

Andy's just returned from his evening appointment with David, and walks into the lounge with a reassuring smile. I feel such a relief now that he's got his extra help on board. He says it's been a real help, but doesn't say very much more, so I don't push him. I just hope it felt like a safe place to talk about how all this is affecting him, without worrying about upsetting me or feeling judged in any way.

Many of us are guilty of bottling our emotions and putting on the well-used 'pretend smile' mask. I admit, I have been just as guilty as the next person, perhaps conscious of burdening others, especially when they may also have things going on in their lives, or maybe just not wanting people to witness our fragile vulnerability.

But life isn't always kind, and unfortunately, no one is exempt from testing times. We will all have those curveballs to dodge at some point in our lives, but from time to time, it might seem as if we've had very little opportunity to recover from the last strike before another one comes along. Whether it be a minor niggle or a gruelling barrage of worries to try and deal with, the body and mind will inevitably begin to tire, and those once reliable resources will become noticeably depleted. I know it can feel like a very lonely place because I've been there, but it doesn't have to be. It may feel uncomfortable to try and reach out or accept those well-meant offers of support, in whatever form they come, but I would encourage anyone to take that leap of faith and embrace the benefits that follow, no matter how big or small.

I have to say though, I'm feeling exhausted at going over the same story and answering the same questions with everyone we see. It really isn't anybody's fault and I'm honestly not criticising, as I truly appreciate their genuine concern and need to try and comprehend what's happened, and it's certainly far better than someone crossing the road to avoid me, as I experienced some years ago when I sadly miscarried. I appreciate that finding out that someone you know has a serious illness will cause people to react very differently. By acknowledging, for some, the uncertainty of knowing what to say for fear of causing upset, I am trying hard to take the lead to ease any potential awkwardness. What I am finding especially hard is the need for some – and they are the minority – to know more than I'm clearly willing and able to share right now. No two days are the same right now, and where one day I feel happy to talk and want people to ask me, the next day I feel consumed by it all and it feels like it's taking over my life.

Well hooray, it's Andy's birthday and thanks to the internet, at least I've been able to order a present for him, as I've certainly not had the chance to go out and get anything recently. We've not exactly got any of the usual plans in place as I have an appointment to have my bloods checked this morning, and then we are off to the hospital's Cancer Centre to meet my oncologist. We are both completely shattered as I don't think either of us have had a wink of sleep, again.

Well, the time has come to head off. It's about 40 minutes' journey, give or take. I can't make conversation in the car; my mind is a fog and I can't think of anything other than what's about to hit us this time. Andy keeps looking at me to check I'm okay. Neither of us can quite believe we're now sitting in a cancer centre waiting to be told what the future holds for us. It feels like we are waiting for absolutely ages as I turn to look at every person that walks in, in case they call out my name. My heart is racing, and I feel so sick inside. My mouth feels like the bottom of a budgie cage, but there's no water fountain in sight and neither of us wants to wander off in case I'm called in.

Next thing, we're invited through to the consulting room. 'Hello, my name is Dr Joe', as he shakes both our hands and offers a lovely warm smile. Inviting us to sit down, he explains that Linsey has been held up, but is on her way. She soon arrives, gently touches our shoulders and asks if we are both okay. He seems to know a lot about my background, where I work and that I previously worked with his colleague Clair. He goes on to say that he hears how highly respected I am by a lot of fellow professionals. That is so lovely of him to say.

Then he asks what we both know to date. As I start to talk, I really don't think my heart can pound any stronger, knowing we're about to be hit with even more life-changing news on top of what we already know. Andy is leaning forward with his elbows on his knees, his hands clasped firmly as he looks at me. We share the confirmation that it is definitely an ovarian cancer, but straight away, Dr Joe says he feels they 'can do something'.

That moment of relief is soon quashed when he proceeds to explain that there is a probable secondary cancer deposit on my liver and a pleural effusion (a build-up of fluid on my lung) and for this reason, they are placing my cancer at Stage 4. Now, to some people that might not appear to mean anything, but to me, that's not good, not good at all!! He says that while this is the case, there is still treatment they can offer, and research is showing some really encouraging results. He follows this with the fact that the cancer will, however, remain incurable. Time has just come to a complete standstill, and the only way I can describe this moment is that my world has just collapsed into totally silent and lonely darkness.

Andy is really struggling with his emotions, but I'm so glad when he starts asking lots of important questions. I'm happy to sit through these, up until he asks about prognosis, clearly a very difficult question for him to ask. This, for me, was a question too far and one I would never want asking. So I stop the conversation in its tracks. Linsey immediately sees how important it is for me not to have this discussion, and kindly intervenes as my advocate. I really didn't want that seed planted in my head, or Andy's; it would haunt us relentlessly for the rest of my life, and I didn't need any more distractions taking anything else away from me. I've cared for so many people given a prognosis and their carers, both with and even without asking. For some, they then become fixated on the time frame and allow it, along with their diagnosis, to define them.

We go on to discuss trials and treatment plans and touch on genetic testing. How on earth do you begin to process such options? None of them are that appealing! I just want someone to tell me which is best for me. Treatment decisions aside, I hadn't even thought about genetic testing and the possibility I might have passed on inherited genes which could predispose Ross and any further generations to cancer. Something else we are going to have to face and gently explore with him.

So, the plan is six cycles (treatment sessions) of a combined chemotherapy with a target therapy, target therapy being a tumour-starving treatment that aims to block and prevent further growth of the blood vessels that feed the tumour. Apparently, after three cycles and regular blood tests, I will have another CT scan to review my treatment response and at this point they will consider if I'm suitable for surgery. The surgery will be major surgery, involving a total abdominal hysterectomy, while also removing my fallopian tubes and omentum. After surgery, I will continue with the remaining cycles of chemo and target therapy. They will continue to discuss my case at the weekly multidisciplinary (MDT) meetings on a Monday morning, looking at my response to treatment and agreeing on my ongoing plan of care. My life remains in their hands.

Before I ask, Dr Joe tells me about the potential and common side effects I could experience and that I should be prepared to lose my lovely hair through the specific chemo I'm going to have. It looks like my private and very personal journey is now going to become a very public one and soon, everyone's going to know what I'm going through. No hair, no eyebrows or eyelashes, I feel no one will see the 'real' me anymore! I know your looks don't define you, but they do tend to reflect who you are.

I'm already envisaging how poorly the treatment is going to make me feel and if I'm going to be able to tolerate it. I can't help picturing friends and patients who have travelled this journey before me and how they have been. It's not getting any better!! Linsey's reassuring presence is so comforting, as she is constantly reading our body language throughout and responding with such warmth, understanding and consideration.

So, with consent forms and pen at the ready, let's get on and kick this thing right up the backside!

# Chapter 5

# The Right Time

Today I have had two phone calls. The first one was offering me a day case admission for another drainage in a couple of days' time. The second one was to invite me for my induction to the chemotherapy unit (CTU) next Monday and to book me for my first chemotherapy treatment on the Friday. It's all moving so quickly, of which I'm glad, but equally I'm getting a bit frightened now, frightened of the unknown. My stomach is churning a bit more each day at the thought of the chemo and how I'm going to be with the side effects.

Andy and I have been chatting about work, and he thinks I should go in and tell everyone now I have all the facts and a plan. When I say everyone, I mean my direct work colleagues on the Inpatient Unit. It's weird, but I actually feel strong enough to go and do this today, but do it my way and not work's way. After all, this is my news to give.

We head over unannounced, and make our way up to my manager's office. Having updated her of everything to date, I tell her we've deliberated and come to the decision that I should tell the staff today, and the response comes back, 'But you don't have the histology results yet, do you not think you should wait'? Well, my decision certainly hadn't been something I had rushed into, and it wasn't something I was entirely at ease with, but I needed to tell my 'friends and work family' before they inadvertently heard it from someone else, perhaps by bumping into one of my close friends or family. Clearly disagreeing, she accepts my decision and without giving a follow-on offer to join us and provide some support, either to ourselves or the staff, Andy and I head off downstairs to 'the girls' to do it together.

The trust and friendships we build through life are something no one else can fully understand. What holds those relationships together is a unique connection of mutual understanding, respect, sharing and giving. I knew my work colleagues and friends so well and was 100%

sure this was the right time to be sharing my news with them, histology or no histology.

Helen's in the office alone. She was working with me on my last night prior to going to the doctor, so she had an idea my absence was likely to be related. She asks how I am, so I break the news to her whilst the three of us are alone. She's simply devastated. I explain that I want to speak to all the staff on duty and with it being handover time, I was likely to get a good group of staff together in one go. She gathers everyone together, ensuring there is only staff I work closely with and not the less familiar staff, such as bank staff and temporary OTs that I don't really know quite as well.

There is a sense of anxiety in the room as both Andy and I are sitting there to greet everyone. Here comes the next shock wave! I stay calm and explain everything as honestly as I can. Reactions are understandably of shock and upset. Some are trying to remain composed as the questions start to come, and that's fine. I encourage them to ask anything, especially as I want them to know all the symptoms, so I can educate and hopefully protect both them and others from this awful disease.

Our GP David's wife Sue is on duty and in the office with us. I turn to her and tell her that David knows. She doesn't need to say this, but still she reassures me that she knew nothing, and I have no doubt that he would ever have discussed me with her. She comes back with how grateful she and everyone is for us both coming to talk to them with such honesty and strength, and reassured us both of all their love and support in the days ahead.

Well, it's finally another drainage day! Again, breathless and fatigued, I'm just managing the stairs one step at a time, clinging on tightly to the banister as I go. Andy drops me off at the main entrance and goes to park. I've managed to get myself into the foyer and quickly parked myself into one of those 'I have a mind of my own' wheelchairs again. To be fair, the wheelchairs are not that easy to grasp, but when you link them together with the possible drivers of the 'abandoned cars' in the car park, it's an entertaining sight everywhere you look.

All booked in and I'm soon taken down to the same clinical room as last time, and taken aback by the lovely welcome, as if I'm an old friend popping in. As the doctor scans my tummy, I watch on and from my other side, I feel a welcome hand cupped over mine. The team are so professional, but still engage in some welcome humour and that suits me, a fellow joker, just fine. I can't help but show a piece of me, as I smile and tell the doctor in a humouring kind of voice, 'You've done very well', as he quickly responds with, 'That's lucky, as it's the first time I've done one of these', and we all have a good chuckle.

Six hours and ten litres later, I'm holding Andy's hand this time, squeezing tightly as I prepare myself for the drain to be removed. Trying so hard to relax my body, I can't help but worry if it's going to be as painful as the last one! 'Take some nice steady breaths for me. There we are, it's out.' Andy takes a deep breath and just says 'Blimey', as that was the first time he had seen one being removed. I have to say, it wasn't nice, but nowhere near as bad as my previous one. I think that's probably because it's only been in for a short period of time. Comfortable once again, I'm off home. Oh joy, strip washes again for two days!

What a fab night's sleep, a lovely lie-in and then another breakfast in bed. Andy tells me he's made another hair appointment for me to get my hair washed and blow-dried this afternoon. I'm so grateful as Ross and Nic are due back today, so I want to look reassuringly 'well' for them. It sounds like they've had an amazing time and the photos are great.

Today we're off to the chemo unit for my induction chat, but before we go, I try to ring Linsey and leave a message, as my fluid is coming back already, after just four days, and I want to try and get it sorted before my chemo on Friday. My appetite is tiny again and I'm feeling tired most of the time (probably because I can't get comfortable to sleep). The stairs remain my daily challenge, in fact a lot seems a challenge at the moment. Anyway, Andy and I have arrived at the chemo unit together, clearly both nervous. We were thinking it was only us having a one-to-one chat, but it's not. There's a group of about eight of us, with partners/ family.

A familiar face very quickly catches my eye: it's Cheryl. We both go back to the 'good old days' when we worked at the hospital. She comes straight over with her lovely bubbly personality and reassuring smile and says, 'Hello lovely', reassuring me I will be fine and that we will have a good chat shortly. We're all invited into a room with recliner chairs and seats, and before the musical chairs starts with the fight for the most comfortable chairs, in her lovely light-hearted way she smiles and tells everyone, 'The comfy chairs are for the patients and the rest of you lot get the less comfy chairs'.

She introduces herself before embarking on a full introduction to what the unit is all about, and explaining how everyone's chemo will be different and respectively tailored, making each person's experience unique to them. Along with our packs and handouts, she covers a range of valuable points, such as potential side effects, sepsis, managing symptoms, our responsibility to monitor our temperatures regularly, and then the 24-hour contact numbers for any advice and emergencies.

Each person then has a one-to-one, a chance to ask questions and discuss any personal worries more privately. With this, I get even more booklets and information on my specific chemo to add to my new 'library'. It's all feeling quite surreal, if I'm quite honest. Next, we're both then shown across to Moira on the Appointments Desk, so she can book me in for my first treatment. Moira is one of the loveliest people I know. Our children went to the same school, and I also know her from my years working at the hospital. She is so empathetic as she offers even more welcome reassurance before we set off home to inwardly digest my collection of handouts.

On our way out, the receptionist stops us and asks if we have a car park token. We did, so she offers to exchange it for another token which apparently entitles us to free car parking. Great, CTU patients get free parking – well, that's a plus at least.

Andy seems a little better about things after that. We chat about what's been said, and he acknowledges how it's helped him to understand things a lot more and that he feels more confident and able to support me now. Perfectly timed, it's not long before Linsey rings back to tell me I'm booked into the day ward at County hospital this time, for another paracentesis in three days' time.

My social calendar for 2020 is leaving a lot to be desired. Two days later, we're off for bloods and a urine test first and then onto Stoke Hospital again, but this time for a nuclear medicine scan. Slowly walking into the department, I'm relieved to be able to sit down whilst Andy speaks to the receptionist. Once called in, I'm soon cannulated and ready to be injected with radioactive dye. As they run the Geiger counter over me, I'm expecting to be radiating a gorgeous yellow glow before too long!

We now need to wait some time before I have to go back again for the second part of the test. With my bloated tummy, I'm far too uncomfortable to sit for any length of time, especially in the very busy main entrance area of the hospital, so we choose to sit, in fact recline the seats in the car, until it's time to go back. Both of us set our alarms just in case we nod off, but it's pouring down and we don't manage much of a nap, to be honest. Then, before too long we're back in again and it's all done relatively quickly.

Soon home again for a sleep on the settee – well, that's if I can get comfortable. Andy gets comfy and it's really not long before we've both nodded off for a good couple of hours. Now close to teatime, I really don't feel like anything to eat tonight, which always unsettles Andy. He tries to tempt me with a variety of options. In the end I opt for a Chicken Cup-a-Soup, mainly to appease him.

I've been feeling quite emotional for most of today, but can't really say why. I know Andy is often watching me when he thinks I'm not looking; it's the same most nights, when we're in bed, as every move I make wakes him so easily and he asks, 'Are you okay?' So when I'm feeling like this, I try so hard to hold it in, as his mind must be all over the place and I don't want to keep adding to his worries if I can help it. I know it's not good for me, but I need to try and look after him too. That's just what I do!

The next day I'm admitted for yet another drainage. Andy takes me in but isn't allowed to stay this time, as I'm sharing a four-bed ward today. Two of the ladies are both two days post-op from having hysterectomies and trust me, I'm already logging what they can do at day two, ready for when it's 'hopefully' my turn. But with the emergency call bell going off for one of the ladies, who had collapsed in the bathroom before being rushed back and transferred onto her bed, it wasn't the best of introductions.

The other lady in the bay was a day case too. She was very chatty and clearly nervous, turning and asking me if I was having a caesarean!! She was absolutely mortified when she realised I wasn't, and not happy to leave it at that, she was even more so when she asked the reason behind me looking pregnant. I tried to play it down to help reduce her embarrassment, but inside I was feeling equally embarrassed and, unsurprisingly, even more self-conscious than before.

The staff in the Imaging room are so lovely as usual. With the procedure becoming increasingly familiar and certainly less daunting, I am just so glad I'm there, having it done. A lovely lady offers her hand as we chat about my journey to date and before we know it, the initial discomfort has passed, the drain is in and I'm draining once again.

Before we leave the room, 'Claire' comes in and introduces herself, as we have only ever spoken on the phone before. She is responsible for organising all the appointments, and clearly knowing of my previous admissions, offers to book me in again in a week's time to avoid me worrying about getting near to crisis point again. I can't tell you how much that meant that she would do that. Unsure if I would need an appointment then, I was mindful that I was not going to take up a valuable place for someone equally in need. She reassured me, saying she would ring me next week, the day before, and see how I was. If I didn't need to come in, she said they would review me and possibly reschedule for the week after if needed.

It was eight litres this time and I'm feeling something like 'normal', whatever 'normal' is, once again. The volumes seem to be gradually reducing, which is reassuring. It's been a long day, so once home, we're both straight to bed. I'm shattered, we're both shattered, and I have my first chemo first thing in the morning.

# Chapter 6

# Here it Goes

My heart is pounding as we both walk into the reception area, still not quite believing I'm attending CTU and, more so, as a patient today. Despite my experience as a general and palliative care nurse, I never spent any time working with chemotherapy treatments. I can hold my hand up and say I understood some of the common side effects and how to manage them, but had no idea of the scope of treatments, their management, specific side effects and what was involved in giving everyone their individual treatments.

Understandably, the first visit into any unknown is extremely daunting. Sitting in a chemotherapy unit waiting area, feeling like I do, whilst being a nurse with some basic understanding and insight, I can only imagine what it must feel like to a lay person. But I'm not sure right now if a little knowledge is any better or worse than no knowledge at all. Quietly sitting there, knowing I'm about to start a course of treatment that is going to involve 'poisoning' my body, my thoughts are distracted by the inevitable, unanswerable questions of whether my body and mind will be able to take this gruelling treatment, along with the uncertainty of whether it will give me what we are all hoping for.

I've already been taunted by my lack of knowledge, wondering how long it's going to be before I start to feel unwell from the side effects once the treatment is started, and if I'm going to be able to cope with them. Looking around the waiting area, apart from one lady with wisps of hair covering her delicate head and another with a chemo hat on, strangely everyone looks in pretty good health and relaxed. Feeling very self-conscious, I can't help but wonder if they see my imaginary flashing light on my head telling them all I'm a 'chemo virgin'.

It's not too long before I get called through with Andy, and I'm led to a recliner chair looking out into the garden area. Andy sits beside me on his 'less comfy' chair, clearly anxious, but trying to be my steadying rock. It's now only a matter of minutes away before I hand control over; with the tray of syringes on the table and my drip stand and pump next to me, all set up, here it goes. The nurse is lovely and takes the time to explain everything to us. With my arm on a pillow, I'm soon cannulated, the portable computer is wheeled across and everything is double-checked between the nurses, myself and my prescription. Firstly, I'm given a cocktail of intravenous drugs, referred to as my 'pre-med' (pre-treatment medication), which are apparently routinely given prior to certain chemotherapy drugs. One of the drugs is Dexamethasone, a steroid given to help control acute nausea and vomiting. The nurse says this can give the sensation of 'a tingly bottom' as she slowly injects it into my cannula. I wait in anticipation but can't say I feel particularly tingly-bottomed right now.

Once I've been given all the drugs, the saline infusion is started and it looks like we are off. Through the day, and it is all day, I have several saline drips run between my chemo infusions. The chemo comes with a coloured bag covering to protect it from the light. I've been feeling fine up to this point, but the one drug has started to make my forearm ache quite a lot. As advised, I let the nurse know and she puts a heat pad over my arm to ease the discomfort, reassuring me this is a common side effect of this drug, and asks me to let her know if it doesn't ease, but gladly it did eventually pass.

Looking around, the unit is quite busy, so my nurse has a few of us to look after, flitting from one to another. You can get up and walk to the toilet if you need to. You just need to disconnect the charge cable from the pump and off you go, with your 'dance partner' (drip stand) by your side. I've been watching a lady across from me and I can't help but wonder if she is the lady Nic knows, called Rosie. If it is, she's on her second cycle today. On my way back from the toilet I pluck up the courage to ask her name, really hoping I'm right. Straight away she says, 'Oh, are you Julia?' We get chatting a little before I return to my chair. She is lovely. Her hair is beautiful and I'm thinking how sad that she's going to lose it all. Little did I know at the time, this was in fact an NHS wig!! It was so authentic-looking. I'm so glad I've met her today and hope we see each other again, so we can chat more.

I take a minute to actually take in what is happening around me. Staff are constantly on the go, but still make time to sit and offer some valuable and very welcome reassurance. There is a constant flow of people coming and going, with others here for the day, like me. Some sit quietly, reading a book or doing puzzles, others are either chatting or making the most of a little nap, and then there are those that have the day to do all three. It's a strange feeling and one that must sound quite bizarre, but I already feel safe here, sharing my time with likeminded people, unknowingly offering appreciation and understanding as we share our journeys together.

More familiar faces all pop in to see me, which is so lovely. I've known them all for years and some of us even go back to the late 80s/early 90s at the hospital – and no, that's not quite Florence Nightingale's era! My visits have really helped to break up our day and prove a welcome distraction for us both. It's about 16:35 and finally, my first session has come to a close. What a long, but strangely reassuring, day for us both.

With my cannula removed, I'm presented with a goodie bag full of 'surprises'. Most of them are drugs that I've got to take for the next three days, to help with the effects of the chemotherapy. I also get a referral to the district nurses and a box of injectable anti-sickness medication, Metoclopramide, which I will need to store in the home in case it's needed. And that's not it! I'm also handed a couple of cards –

well, when I say cards, I don't mean 'Congratulations on your first treatment' cards, I actually mean a blue steroid treatment card and a yellow cancer treatment card to carry with me whenever I am out. The yellow card is my 'Get me out of the waiting area' card to inform professionals that I am undergoing cancer treatment and because of this, I have priority health needs. Oh, and I nearly forgot, I also have a bloods form and urine bottle to complete my array of 'goodies'.

I can't quite believe how great I feel, given how I had imagined I would feel. I'd not felt this great in a good while, and that's with my first dose of chemo on board!!! I can only assume it's down to the huge dose of steroids I've been given pre-chemo.

The next few days have been somewhat mixed. Generally, I have a wonderful appetite, despite feeling nauseated and heaving over my lovely mixing bowl all night, with the occasional vomits. But with one of my post-chemo medications that helps manage nausea and vomiting, I also succumb to one of its unwelcome side effects, constipation. So, with this delight, I now have to add a lovely selection of laxatives to my cocktail of daily medications, and force myself to drink much more. Neither of us have any energy or enthusiasm to do a great deal as we were so sleep-deprived, and I'd had better days, to be honest, so we just sit and watch some daytime TV. Then arrived our first meals on wheels, care of my brother-in-law and his wife… a full Sunday roast. It was amazing and soon polished off, and it wasn't long before we were ready for an afternoon nap, again!

Next comes the neuropathic pain, which has started in my legs. It's a pain like I've never experienced before. I just spent hours rubbing my legs, unable to find any position comfortable for more than two minutes, and as for the nights, poor Andy, it was like sleeping with someone trying to wrestle a crocodile for much of the night. I need a pillow between my knees, that's better, oh no I don't want the pillow now, oh I do need a pillow again... constantly for the next 3–4 days.

After finishing my three days of post-chemo steroids, I can only describe the feeling as though my body had just crashed into a brick wall. Total exhaustion, loss of appetite, persistent neuropathic pain and an overwhelming sense of fatigue. My tummy was expanding again and that only meant one thing, and I hit breaking point, big style. I was so incredibly tired, but my legs still wouldn't allow me to sleep. I tried so hard not to disturb Andy as he was exhausted too, but the tears started to roll, and I just couldn't hold back the 'perfect storm' any longer. He was so good, awake in seconds and there with his reassuring words and a cuddle. The tears didn't really slow very much, but there were moments that allowed us to talk. Every possible scenario was going round in my head, and they all just needed to be vented.

Covid is making itself increasingly apparent across the world, with our TVs relentlessly dominated by updates and horrendous rising death tolls. It's so unbelievably sad and depressing for everyone. People are understandably on edge, but there are still the 'invincible ones' whose scepticism is worrying. It's my sister-in-law's $60^{th}$ birthday party this weekend, and as much as I would love to go, I really can't risk picking anything up, especially when I am currently in the high-risk phase of being susceptible to neutropenic sepsis. I think everyone is respecting my decision, but I'm not sure they fully understand why I am being so cautious. Albeit with some anxiety, I persuade Andy to go. He really needs to switch his head off for a while and just enjoy a bit of socialising.

So, it's another admission today and another lovely welcome from everyone. Drain in once more and I ask the consultant how many times he feels I will need to come in again before things start to settle completely. He thinks I may need another 2–3 drains over the next month and by then, he's hoping the chemo should have dried most of it up, if not all. To hear that was such a relief and a positive focus for me.

The poor nurses were back and to, either doing my observations or emptying my bag. I hated having to press my nurse call button, so I would wait until the bag was near full before I bothered them. A lovely student nurse, who had been given the responsibility of managing my observations for several hours, came to empty my bag the one time. Equipped with her papier maché bedpan, she opened the tap and after about 400 mls, it appeared to be running everywhere. Unknowingly, the bedpan had a tiny hole in it. I felt so sorry for her, she didn't know what to do first. The time seemed to pass so slowly, so this was a short moment of unfortunate entertainment, which had everyone rushing about to help her. She looked mortified, so I tried to reassure her that I had seen this happen on several occasions in my time as a nurse, and how funny it was to see the panic hit with little time to react.

It wasn't long after this that I had such a lovely welcome surprise: Sue, one of the doctors from work, walked into the bay. She had popped out of work just to see me and that had meant so much, as I knew how precious her time was, yet she had still had me in her thoughts and plans for today. She also came bearing carefully considered gifts too, which was so thoughtful of her, making me smile inside and out.

# Chapter 7

# Introduced to Neutropenic Sepsis

It's been a lovely welcome change, catching up with the girls and being allowed out for a Costa and cake. Life felt a tad normal, for a while at least. It was then back home for a little sleep before tea and then, as if from nowhere, Andy comes in with the thermometer and says, 'Just check your temperature'. The reading was 39.4c and apparently, I looked as if I had just walked out of a sauna. The worrying thing was that I was oblivious; I felt 'fine'. After a quick call to the 24hr helpline on the Emergency Assessment Unit (EAU), it was either a 999 call or if close by, as was the case, head straight up to A&E. With a flash of my yellow card we were taken straight through to a side-room, away from everyone in the waiting area and the possible Covid admissions at the time, all waiting to be triaged.

With my history taken, the needles were coming from all angles. Bloods, blood sugars, cannula, IV fluids and then urine dip and an ECG. It felt like *Emergency Ward 10*! Next it was time for a dose of paracetamol to try and get my temperature down. After about an hour, the bloods were apparently back and the doctor returned to tell me I had a very serious infection. 'You have neutropenic sepsis and we need to transfer you to Stoke Hospital as soon as possible.' I was going to be heading off to the nearest major hospital for my ongoing management. In the interim I have my first dose of IV antibiotics and an injection of Filgrastim, which is given to boost the production of white cells to help me fight infection. Having turned midnight, I tell Andy to go home and get some rest, as he too is shattered.

After a couple of brief power naps, I'm woken by three ambulance crew standing at the end of my trolley with a stretcher. They look both cold and tired as they announce that my chariot awaits. They ask if I need help to transfer to the stretcher but I manage to get across, drips and all, before they wrap me up in blankets, strap me in and out into the cold we go. With yet more observations completed, the crew reference a code (for sepsis patients), before advising me we will be travelling on 'blues and twos' all the way in. This is a first, as I have been an observing crew on several 999 calls in the past, but never been the strapped-in patient, abnormally, travelling backwards.

Travelling with pace, I hear a blast of the horn. It's now around 01:30 and very dark out there, so I can't imagine what that was for. When we arrive at the hospital, the driver explains why he'd needed to blast his horn. It turned out to be two 'idiots' dressed in camouflage, on their Harley Davidsons, driving with no lights on down a poorly-lit stretch of road. I said, 'I guess you will be going back to scoop them up later then?' The driver replied, 'More than likely, that's if we can find them with all that camouflage on'.

I'm soon checked in, with the crew told I'm going into side room 3. We arrive at room 3, only to find an elderly gent is lying there! The crew ask again, to be told by the staff nurse they had meant to move the gentleman out before I arrived. The crew and I have a little giggle as the staff move the gentleman out. The one says, 'I know the NHS are stretched, but that's perhaps a tad too cosy'. I replied with 'I'm a pretty sociable person, but just not THAT sociable!' Once settled into my newly vacated side room, the crew ensure I'm going to be alright before they leave. I thank them and hope they have a good night.

With more ongoing observations, history taking, IV fluids and antibiotics and a very uncomfortable trolley, there was not much sleep to be had. A lovely empathetic doctor comes onto the morning shift, and we discuss my treatment plan and the fact that I also have another drainage booked for tomorrow. She explains that they are waiting on a side room to become available on the ward and that the oncology CNSs are apparently hot on the case for me, but with the ever-increasing numbers of Covid admissions, this may take time. I don't think I can stay on that trolley any longer and ask if I could be swapped onto a bed, so I can get comfortable and rest. She smiles and says, 'Oh, of course I can, I will get the nurses to organise one for you'. It's not long before my lovely bed arrives and in comparison, it's sumptuous.

Eventually I'm transferred to the EAU in the Cancer Centre. I'm there barely 10 minutes before I'm whisked off for a drainage. I really hadn't expected that to be arranged so quickly, but at the same time I'm so grateful. When I get back Andy is there with my overnight goodies. It's lovely to have visitors, as side rooms can become lonely places at times. As it turned out, this was to be the last time I could get to see him while I was in hospital, as the Cancer Unit and much of the hospital were stopping all visiting with immediate effect due to the rising Covid figures, both locally and nationally.

That evening I had a visit from a lovely medical student, who introduced himself as Khalid. He asked if he could sit and chat with me about my journey to date. I was more than happy to, especially as I was not likely to be chatting with any visitors of my own anytime soon. He was keen for me to talk about everything right from the start, occasionally asking things such as how I'd dealt with it at that time. He said he was so impressed with how articulate I'd been in explaining everything and was inspired, not only by my spirituality, but also how it was helping me to deal with the whole situation. He said, 'I want to thank you for sharing with me. I really have learnt so much from talking to you and know I will always carry this experience with me throughout my career'. I'm sure if all medics and nurses were permitted the time to sit and chat with their patients in the way Khalid had, which was probably a good hour, we would have a much greater number of insightful professionals, who could explore and benefit from understanding the unique stories that come from a life with cancer.

The days ahead were particularly hard. I'd had endless nights of broken sleep, with high temperatures and rigors, regular observations, endless paracetamol, bedding on and bedding off, early morning bloods, infusion pump alarming and drip changes, IV antibiotics, and to top it all I was starting to notice the amount of hair I was losing. Now tucked away in a huge, new and very bland side room with my door closed, a TV and recliner chair that don't work, no visitors permitted, no means of distraction and my phone flat with no chargers available to borrow, just a silent and lonely room where I felt totally consumed by so many thoughts and emotions, I hit another, this time very solitary, breaking point.

A delightful HCA on nights came in to do my observations and asked how my day had been. I'm sure it was quite apparent I had been crying, but she didn't draw attention to this. She was so lovely and compassionate, saying she would be back shortly. About ten minutes later, the room door opened and she tells me, 'Right, I'm not having you stay in here, we're going to move you across to a different side room. I've just checked for you and the TV and recliner chair both work'. Such a small gesture that gave me a heartfelt boost. The next day, despite being extremely busy, someone very kindly rang Andy, on my behalf, to ask him to bring in a list of things for me, but we still wouldn't be able to see each other.

As if the sepsis and no visitors weren't enough, it was so painful to now see and feel my hair coming out by the handful. Thank goodness I've asked Andy to pack my hat to put on if needs be. I'm mindful that I'm going to look like a 'cancer patient' once I pull that on, and that everyone who now sees me with it on will be thinking, 'She's got cancer' and I must be bald. I really don't know why I'm worrying about that as I am in the Cancer Centre at the end of the day, and it won't really come as a shock to them, will it?! I talked with one of the staff nurses on nights and she was so empathetic. She even shared with me how she had experienced alopecia a few years ago and how it had affected her.

The Oncology CNS has just called in to see me and advises me I'm going to need an albumin infusion to correct my bloods. She says this is likely to be due to the amount of fluid I've drained so far. Asking how my chest is feeling as I have a cough and I'm still a little breathless at times, she refers to the fluid on the left lung that they are already aware of, and how they may consider draining that if it becomes more problematic. Immediately, I'm totally petrified; I can't hold back my tears and really struggle to explain my reaction for a minute or two. My late mother had Amyloidosis, which meant she needed recurrent pleural drainage and eventually a pleurodesis (a procedure which sticks your lung to the chest wall), which she'd said was so painful and severely traumatised her at the time. The very thought of it has brought back an extremely distressing memory from the past. The CNS listens and is very understanding and apologises for upsetting me. She thinks it would be highly unlikely that I would need one, so advises me not to worry anymore.

Just to be safe, I'm told I have virology swabs taken to try and find the cause of my persistent temperature and cough. Little did I know that this was my initiation into what would become years of Covid swabbing procedures. Once done, it's now time for my drain to be removed, and as before, this one has been in for days.

The CNS brings along a staff nurse who wants to observe a drain being removed. I was so glad she was there, as it was definitely well and truly stuck and the pain was absolutely horrendous. It truly felt like my insides were being ripped out! Although the staff nurse hadn't eased my pain, her support has been greatly appreciated. My CNS was so apologetic and I think shocked that it was so difficult for her to remove. Although somewhat traumatised, I'm finally no longer attached and I'm 7 litres lighter. I can once again get around independently and it feels so liberating.

The day has arrived, and I'm being discharged home, finally able to see Andy and my family once again. Every single member of staff has been incredible: catering staff, nurses, HCAs, housekeepers, medics, all taking such good care of me, and always making every effort to lift my spirits with a smile and sometimes the smallest of kind gestures. They were all working through what was to be just the start of such uncertain times, putting their lives on the line for people such as me. I have been praising them to their faces daily and make sure, as I leave, that I tell them all again, and again. They deserve to see and hear that recognition and gratitude, to bolster their self-belief and worth.

It feels great and I'm so grateful to be going home again. As I walk through the front door, Trigger is so happy to see me; I think he thought I wasn't coming back. He is so intuitive to me not being well, like many dogs that pick up on illnesses such as diabetes and cancers. Apparently, they can tune into a distinctive faint odour that's impossible for humans to detect. For example, whenever I'm sat or lying on the sofa, he's started to want to be up and next to me, snuggled with his nose resting against my tummy, and when I'm in bed he has started to lie under my side of the bed, something he's never done before either.

With my chemo now delayed by a few weeks and extended periods between treatment, I'm going to make the most of my free time and make some cakes for the family. I can't go anywhere, because as of yesterday, the UK has gone into an official 'lockdown,' and I'm now deemed an 'extremely vulnerable person.' Both Andy and I are having to shield for the time being, as we can't afford to pick anything up by going out and mixing with others either.

So, like so many, we are stuck in our albeit lovely home, forced to have anyone who comes round stand outside the front window, talking to us through the glass. If ever there was a time to want a simple hug from family and friends, I can tell you, it's now. Those that know me well know that I'm a tactile person who loves to give and receive hugs. I'm not entirely wrapped up in my own world and I'm certainly very aware of how everyone is finding themselves affected by this awful virus, and how many of them will also be needing hugs, but if ever there was a time not to start a cancer journey, for me, that time is now.

Today's another massive day for me: it's my appointment at the wig shop to have my 'once beautiful' hair shaved off, one of my worst nightmares. My head has been so painful and sore at times, probably from the weight of my hair pulling on the inflamed hair follicles as it's continued to come out by the handful. I wake each morning and my pillow's covered in hair, my clothes end up covered and I'm hoovering up hair daily. Andy desperately wants to be there at the wig shop to support me, and I really need him to be there, but because of lockdown he's not allowed in and I have to go it alone. I'm only allowed there as it's part of my treatment plan.

I've now accepted that I can't carry on as I have been and the inevitable isn't going to go away. We chat for a while before agreeing what I want her to do. When I say ‘want’, I think I actually mean ‘need’. She keeps the mirror uncovered, at my request, so I can see as she goes along. None of it is going to be pleasant, but I certainly don’t fancy a ‘grand finale’. As she picks up her scissors, the hair clippers by her side, I look at myself in the mirror with a heavy heart as she makes the first cut. My once beautiful hair starts to fall to the floor and onto my gown and I really don’t know how to react. Inside, I’m truly heartbroken as I can’t see ‘me’ anymore; that person in the mirror isn’t me, she’s a total stranger. I’m now thinking that if I see a stranger, will I be a stranger to everyone else and will even my family and friends forget the Julia inside, distracted by this unwelcome transformation? I think it was at this defining point that the reality of me being a cancer patient really hit home.

Once she’d finished, she gets me to put my wig on. There is a tiny hint of me again, with my wig very similar to my original hair. I feel so self-conscious as I walk out of the shop. Andy, who was asleep in the car, says it’s ace...’It just looks like your own hair’, and I'm still thinking, ‘I bet everyone is thinking, “that looks like a wig”’. My dear friend also had a wig which she apparently called Matilda, but I’m struggling to think of a name for mine at the moment. After a few hours at home, I psych myself up to taking the wig off so Andy can get to see the 'bald me'. He tells me it really suits me short. Well, there's short and there's really SHORT. One thing I'm sure of is that I don't really want Ross to see me without my hair. I keep thinking back to their wedding last August when I looked and felt so amazing. That's the image of his mum I want him to be thinking of each day, not how I'm looking right now.

# Chapter 8

# Back on Track

Last night we had our first 'Clap for Carers' at 20:00, a token gesture of appreciation offered to acknowledge the commitment and dedication of the NHS staff who were selflessly providing under such unprecedented times. I wasn't feeling brave enough to go outside so I stood at the lounge window and clapped, with the window open so I could hear everyone taking part. It was quite emotional to see and hear, as Andy stood at the garden wall clapping and waving to everyone and all my immediate neighbours were waving across at me. It felt only right to then ring work to tell the girls I'd been clapping for them too.

Everyone's lives and plans were on hold as the world tried to protect itself from the relentless devastation being created by this merciless virus. No one was exempt, but some were still defiant, showing little concern for the potential consequences of their actions. Although horrendous, I coped with my isolation by accepting that whilst tucked away, we were as safe as we could be, but still so fearful for my friends and family. We had a steady flow of wonderful gestures from everyone: flowers, gifts, cards and letters, homemade cakes, all 'made with love'. It was so humbling.

The next month saw me take on the chemo once again, and with no visitors permitted on the unit, I was suitably equipped with my Kindle, Sudoku puzzles, sweets and headphones. It is so hard to explain to anyone who has not been through chemo, but I actually looked forward to my treatment days. It always felt like a safe place to me, surrounded by people who understood 'the journey'. Everyone seems so mindful of each other, reading each other's body language before engaging in any conversations and sometimes, just a smile is enough. With others, we're chatting, sharing puzzle books and magazines, having a laugh with the nurses, and the next minute we're grabbing that desperately needed nap that we perhaps didn't realise we needed. As with most things in life, there's always one. One who has no concept of body language and just wants to tell every bit of their story to date and demonstrate how well 'they know' the nurses. Fortunately, I only had one morning with one of our 'exhausting friends'.

With a new plan in place this time, my chemo was scheduled four-weekly instead of three, allowing my body longer to recover in between. I would also need to inject myself with the Filgrastim every day, for the next three days after each cycle. Having spent my whole career giving people various kinds of injections, or teaching them how to inject themselves, I couldn't then not rise to this latest challenge. There was no way Andy was going to give it to me – he would be on the deck before I had even taken the injection out of the fridge. So again, I pulled my big girl's pants up, gave myself a talking to and just got on with it. Rather that than another bout of sepsis and my treatment set back even more.

It didn't take long to establish an understanding of how my body reacted to each cycle of chemo. Without a doubt, I would need to scrap any kind of plans for the first week at least. Not that anyone was able to go and do or plan anything at that time anyway. With more of the same side effects, I learnt to mentally prepare, always reassuring myself that in X number of days this will start to ease and that will have passed. However, with the new Filgrastim injections, I wasn't prepared for the drug to exacerbate the neuropathic pain in the way it did, only gradually subsiding after about 6–7 days.

Most of my days were spent doing very little really – jigsaws, mindfulness colouring books and taking regular co-codamol from my mother-in-law's stash of unwanted pills. I know, that's naughty, and with me being a nurse I should know better, but I would like to think, even with 'chemo brain', that I 'kinda know what I'm doing'. The one thing that I could really lose myself in was researching and building my family tree. I even did online courses in genealogy, which enabled me to understand the obstacles that I would come across as I went further and further back.

Having learnt to accept the transient bad days, it was always so lovely to reach day 8–9, a time when I would be starting to feel considerably better. After just two cycles of chemo there was a huge noticeable difference in the amount of ascites I was draining, and I was finally starting to think that this might be the last time I'm going to need it dealing with. My monthly bloods were so encouraging, proving my cancer was responding well to the treatment, and all the anguish I had endured so far had not been in vain.

It's my birthday, my first ever experience of a ‘lockdown birthday’. Despite the imposed restrictions on everyone, many of my family and friends pop by, leaving their cards and gifts in the porch like courier drop-offs, just without the obligatory photo for proof of delivery. They stand at the lounge window and we try to chat, simply making the most of just seeing each other. It’s so strange!

With a knock at the back gate, Andy appears to know who it might be. It’s my wonderful friends Shereen and Syd, laden with boxes and ‘things’. We’re told to go in for now whilst I watch in amazement as they set up a beautiful afternoon tea for Andy and myself. We have lovely vintage china and a delicious array of food for the cake stand, even some non-alcoholic fizz. With bunting now hanging across the fence panels, the table is finished off with beautiful daffodils placed in a vintage china jug. I’m simply blown away and quite emotional as we take in their heartfelt gesture. With guidelines preventing us from being outside together, they invite us to simply enjoy. Once they have left, Andy and I sit down and take in the views down the garden and into the field. We look at each other and smile, make a toast and humbly embrace the moment.

Woohoo, it's shopping delivery day today. We make fun of the fact that this has become the highlight of the week. We have to just stand at the window and acknowledge the driver as he puts everything in the porch. I open the window enough to call out a thank you before he collects up his baskets and leaves, giving me a smile and thumbs up. How sad that there's an element of excitement as we struggle to remember quite what we've ordered. Andy empties the bags as I find homes for everything before we both wash our hands thoroughly, again!!

A few days have passed and as very few people can have face-to-face appointments currently, I chat with my consultant over the phone. He reminds me that usually, after cycle three they would be doing a repeat scan, checking my Ca 125 and planning for surgery, but because of Covid-19 there are no plans for any elective surgery for the foreseeable future. He thinks I will therefore need to continue with a total of six cycles before surgery is likely to be planned, and that's another four months away.

You know what, there's absolutely nothing I can do or say that is going to change anything. I had been able to logically plot my journey in my head and had mentally prepared myself for the surgery in front of me, but now, with Covid devastating and destroying lives and dominating the NHS resources so many take for granted, I've got no other option than to accept it. I realise I'm one of thousands facing the same news, but that really doesn't offer much comfort right now.

Well, onto the next cycle of chemo and lovely company. The lady opposite me is having the 'cold cap' treatment to try and preserve her hair as much as possible. I really admire her stoicism as she bears the expected but uncomfortable sensation of a severe ice cream headache or brain freeze for the first 10–15 minutes. Apparently, once the freezing has taken place it does start to feel less uncomfortable.

It's funny, but no one really gives thought to how enforced hair loss can impact men too, but it does. The difference is that men are generally less comfortable talking about it, perhaps because they are inevitably more likely to experience hair loss in their lives than women, and therefore feel that the impact for them will seem to be far less significant. When I asked, a male nurse on the unit told me how the men tend to speak to him about their concerns more than the female staff, and that it can often be the butt of friends' jokes, especially when suggesting toupees.

So, tonight's our first ever family virtual quiz night and a welcome distraction for me, as I'm on Day Four and in quite a lot of pain still: 'The Big Fat Isolation Quiz 2020', with Ross and Nic as our quizmasters for the night and six other teams of family members, both far and near. It's been such a giggle and the time's gone so quickly. I can't believe we've been quizzing for nearly two hours, as Ross announces the prize for this week's winners. I hasten to add, it's not us winning the box of sweeties this week. Thinking it'll be a good distraction for the week ahead, I volunteer to do the quiz questions for next Friday's quiz. We come offline and both say how lovely it's been, and such a refreshing change to our usual evenings just lately.

# Chapter 9

# My Prayers have been Heard

The phone rings and I recognise that number; it's the hospital. My heart rate has just shot up again as I'm certainly not due a call. With all the hype in the media over Covid's impact on NHS resources, I'm worried sick that they're now going to tell me I can't have my chemo either. It was Clair, as she tells me she's with Miss San, the gynaecology consultant I met back in February. She goes on to explain that they have been in a meeting to discuss cancer patients awaiting a date for surgery, as the Trust are currently in a better position to start offering elective surgery again. I'm going to need another CT scan within the next two weeks and from the results they will then review everyone and plan to prioritise each case. She thinks that, if the scan is as expected, my surgery is likely to proceed within the next 4–6 weeks. My focus is back and I can again try and prepare for the next stage.

Last night we did the weekly family virtual quiz again. I was still in so much pain from persistent aches after my last chemo which have left me particularly low in mood, albeit still focused, but with the advantage of being virtual I can still take part and just embrace the competition and laughter between everyone. It was better than just moping on the sofa feeling sorry for myself.

The shielding restrictions are starting to challenge me a bit now. Cabin fever is pretty testing at the best of times, but when you're going through this kind of journey and you can't have your family and friends beside you, to just hold you and give you that much-needed hug to help release your hidden tears, it's so incredibly hard. Standing on the other side of a window talking to someone, you don't really get a comfortable conversation flowing and you're always aware that your so-called private conversation is open for anyone walking by to overhear. When I get 'window visitors' popping round, I'm always asked how I'm doing and people tell me I look great, which is lovely. But with the barrier of the window between us and the inability to chat properly, I often find myself putting on a front for fear of my emotions getting the better of me, so I simply smile and tell them I'm fine.

I've been thinking a lot about the fact that Andy's not been on his road bike for ages now and I know how much he's missing it, both for his physical and mental well-being. I've been feeling so guilty because my shielding has meant he's had to stop doing what he loves too. After chatting with some friends the other night, I suggest he goes out for some solo rides, just locally. He's unsure as he doesn't want to compromise my vulnerability or leave me in case I feel unwell whilst he's out. Finally, he agrees to give it a go and returns after an hour and a half, having really enjoyed himself. His smile is massive, and he can't stop talking about it.

I really can't remember the last time I slept all night. I think I was absolutely shattered. Last night we were watching *Britain's Got Talent* and a mother, along with her fourteen-year-old daughter, came on stage to audition. The judges do their usual, 'Tell us a bit about you and why you're here'. The daughter explained that her mother had been going through a cancer journey for the past two years and how special it was to be able to be with her on stage 'tonight'. Well, that was it for me, with my heart feeling like it's breaking, I struggle to push back my emotions and break down in tears. Andy comes over to me and gives me a big hug. I think, with my last markers still very much on my mind, telling me what a fight I have ahead of me, all this was just too relatable for me.

Before I join him in bed, I'm drawn to quietly look at our beautiful wedding album Ross and Nic gave us as a keepsake from their wedding. Perhaps not the best thing to do when you've been so upset, but I couldn't help it. I wanted to look at the memories they will have of me before cancer and remember who I once was. Whilst the memories make me smile inside and out, I can't help but cry when I look at myself 'as I was'. I felt so beautiful, confident and happy on that day and so many people said I looked absolutely stunning. I wonder when, or if, I will feel this way again and when, or if, people will again think, 'She's beautiful'.

The mind can be so cruel sometimes. I'm convinced people will no longer see the true me because of how drastically my looks have changed. I am still very much me, albeit going through an external transformation, but feeling inside as if I'm slowly and painfully being stripped of my more familiar and precious identity. All too quickly, I feel trapped in this new persona, an image that would prevent people from recognizing the 'old me', who was still very much alive.

It's my CT appointment this morning and I'm in and out again in no time. So today we just chill and do very little. The weather's changed from yesterday's lovely sunshine, which is nice as I can sit in the garden without having to worry about the sun burning me, as they recommend you stay out of direct sunlight to avoid burning when you are on chemo. We sit and have lunch outside and then I read a bit of my Kindle and do some patterns in my colouring book. Andy reads some of his book and it's not long before he's totally relaxed and falls asleep. I'm sure he could fall asleep on a clothesline!

Today, absolutely nothing is going to spoil our day. Nic has her scan at the hospital and with Covid restrictions, partners are not allowed to go in, so Ross will have to sit in the car and wait for her to come out. I'm gutted for them as this is a moment they should be going through together, but he's not alone and we all appreciate that these restrictions are in place to protect both them and the staff. Today is even more special, as they are finding out the sex of the baby. Nic has a plan in place so she can do her own gender reveal for Ross to make it as special as possible. She's got two dresses hidden in her bag, one blue and one pink. Once she knows, she will get changed and walk out to the car and hope he realises she's in a different outfit, of a certain colour!!!

It's so lovely, all our worries have simply gone away today and all I can think about is how excited Ross and Nic must be right now. Nic finally rings to say they're coming round in about half an hour. There's no giveaway as Nic's clearly got changed again. I obviously don't mind what sex the baby is, I just want a healthy and happy grandchild to love always. Nic's parents and brothers arrive and everyone, for the first time in months, congregates in the garden... socially distanced, of course, as I stand well away from everyone. Ross hands out gender reveal scratch cards to us all, making sure we all have our own coin to scratch off, and then they both say 'GO'!! As we're all starting to see what they reveal, there's squeals of joy as they let off their pink confetti cannons. I'm just over the moon for them. They look so wonderfully happy. I'm desperate to give them both a big hug and it's so incredibly painful and hard not to.

My dear Aunty Pam has unexpectedly Facetimed me tonight; it's such a lovely surprise. She is having to shield whilst she too goes through exactly the same treatment as me. I quickly scrabble round in search of my beanie hat before I answer, but I can't find it in time – but I know she'll understand. As I would expect, she soon says 'That's brilliant' and whips off her cap. We very much share the same sense of humour and I say, 'We look like a couple of boiled eggs', and both just have a good belly laugh. We chat about our journeys so far and our pending scans, and just how we're doing in general. It still seems unbelievable that in August last year, at Ross and Nic's wedding, both of us were looking and feeling so well and then, in such a short period of time, we are both diagnosed with ovarian cancer.

As the government restrictions continue, I'm determined not to let the relentless social isolation get to me. I've spent hours on my family tree in the past few days, and managed to go back several generations. It really is a great distraction, enough to say that I even set my alarm on my phone at hourly intervals to prompt me to get up and stretch my legs and make a drink.

Andy's going out for a long ride on his bike shortly, so I'm going to be home alone for two to three hours. I've quietly decided to take advantage of being on my own today, and do something extremely important to me: I'm going to refresh 'my letters', letters I've already written to my family and friends some years ago, to be handed to them in the event of my death. I have always been of the mindset that life is fragile and should never be taken for granted. None of us knows what our future holds, or what's waiting for us as we walk through the paths of life.

To some, this might seem a bit premature and morbid, but I have my late mother and grandmother to truly thank for this. My wonderful grandmother wrote letters for her children to receive in the event of her death. For my mother, it proved to be such a comfort in the days and years ahead, something that inspired her to do the same. When I read my letter, I hear my mother saying those words to me. I treasure it to this day.

With working in a hospice, I have had many situations which have nurtured discussions with patients who are facing limited time. We have talked about letters and the offered comfort behind them, for both the sender and the receiver. For me, sitting and taking notes from someone when they've been too poorly to write for themselves has been an honour and complete privilege. For all those I've written, I always read back before handwriting it into a card for them to sign. I've even shared letters of my own to help offer some guidance for this incredibly emotional gesture.

I remember a lady's son returning to speak to the staff about two weeks after her death; I was on duty that evening. He had things he wanted to understand about when she died which I was able to answer for him, as I had been with her when she died. He also mentioned his letter from his mother and wondered who had actually written it. Again, I could answer that. I reassured him that every word was said by his mother and all I had done was to write it out for her, word for word. He was quite emotional at this point and said how much his letter had meant to him, and thanked me so much for helping her to fulfil her dying wish.

With my letters already written, I'm only going to start and read through them one by one and tweak them, so that they are brought up to the current day. I think I might also put a photograph into some of them. I haven't included my present illness, as I want them to be about my happy memories and my hopes for the future. I remember when I initially wrote my letters, I pretty much cried on and off all the way through and despite this, I felt so relieved to have done them and put them safe for that day... hoping that it would be a long way in the future.

It's been a lovely weekend of baking for everyone and just pottering in the garden and doing 'normal' things. You know, it's the strangest of feelings, as despite this cancer and ongoing treatment, with its unpleasant side effects, I have been feeling well for what 'seems' like ages, which is so welcome. If it wasn't for the lack of hair, I would say this must all have been a horrendous dream.

The next day I'm up early as Dr Joe, my Oncologist, is ringing me around 08:50 for my telephone consultation. It's not been a great night as I'm feeling nervous about what he's going to say today. He'll have my scan results now and these are going to determine if I am suitable for any surgery, or not. I just can't sit still. It's not until nearer 10:00 when the phone eventually rings. I can feel my heart pounding away, and feel like I'm going to be sick. He says, 'Hi Julia, how are you doing?' I make a point of telling him how good I've been feeling over the past weeks, and he genuinely sounds encouraged by this. He confirms he's seen the scan and is happy for me to go ahead with surgery if it's still something I want doing.

Without hesitation, I let him know I do want it doing.

So, I will have my next chemo on 26th May as planned, but without the Avastin, because of its potential to cause bleeding and delay the healing process. I can't have it up to four weeks before and four weeks after surgery. I ask if the surgery is therefore going to be within the next month and he suggests it is likely to be around 10th–12th June, roughly three weeks away. Before he goes, I just want to ask if he would agree to me going for a daily walk with Andy and Trigger. He seems really keen for me to start doing this, both for my physical and my mental well-being. I don't really need telling, but I just need to stay distanced and try to avoid seeing too many people whilst we're out. Before he goes, he asks (as always) how Andy and Ross are and ends the call by wishing me well, saying he will speak with me after a couple of weeks post-surgery, and then schedule me in for further chemo.

I'm so relieved it's going to go ahead soon. It's a scary prospect and not without significant risks, but they're risks I need to accept if I am to be given this chance of my life back. I've started ringing round everyone and telling them the 'good news'. I must ring Aunty Pam to tell her, as she is also at a similar point in her personal journey and will want to know what I've been told. I still find it unbelievable that we are going through all this at the same time, but regrettably, it does mean we can completely understand how each other is feeling and can support one another in a way others can't.

# Chapter 10

# All in Agreement

It's my last chemo day before my surgery and I'm hoping it will be a much shorter day today, with not having the Avastin. Today my chair is socially distanced from a lovely lady called Wendy. Once we are both set up and our infusions are underway, we start to chat together. When you're on CTU, it's amazing how open many people are with complete strangers. Ultimately, we are all there as members of an elite group of people sharing a mutual and empathetic understanding for something I really don't think I'm able to explain to a non-cancer patient. She tells me that this is her first chemo since her operation four weeks ago, and how everything is looking really positive for her. She has ovarian cancer and has recently undergone major surgery, just as I am going to have soon, and looks amazing! I tell her that I too have ovarian cancer and that I'm planned to have the same surgery as her. I think it's fate that has sat us together today. I don't think the staff intentionally plan this kind of thing, as I've sat with people with several different cancers. I've told Wendy how much she has helped and inspired me today and thanked her so much.

Clair kindly pops in to see me, and we have a good talk about the operation and my treatment plan following that. It really is a lot to be processing all at the same time, but I'm someone who likes to know, understand and process, which enables me to prepare.

Today is my mother's birthday – she would have been 88 years old. I think, with not feeling great post-treatment day, I'm also feeling particularly reflective. Ross has been to get some flowers for me so we can take them up to the crematorium. Holding firmly on to Andy's arm, we walk across to the remembrance room, but with us both shielding for so long, neither of us had given it a thought, the room is understandably closed to the public because of Covid. I can't help but get upset, as it's so difficult; this is the first time since her dying that I've not had my quiet time alone with her on her birthday. It feels like I've been hit with yet another emotional blow, but again, I have to accept that I'm not alone in being dealt these rotten cards. I'm one of thousands who are also being denied the freedom to do such simple gestures that are so spiritually important to them. We've decided to take the flowers home and enjoy them as we mark this special day. I know she would have told me to do the same.

The following day, the weather being so lovely and Andy picking up on my mood, he suggests going for a spin in the car to break up the day. We simply drive around nearby villages, spotting some stunning properties as we just look in envy. We end up at Blithfield Reservoir, sitting, chatting, having an ice cream and just watching the world go by. It's these small gestures that really do make all the difference.

My life has become dictated by appointments, tests and treatments. I have yet another appointment this afternoon and this is with the gynaecology consultant who I'm expecting to consent me for my operation. But it's another wobbly day, as I'm also worrying that they may cancel my operation because of Covid continuing to run amuck.

We sit in the waiting area along with another couple. The lady looks so fragile, with her little wisps of hair resting on her bald head and an Alice band, I feel so much for her. She looks so vulnerable and sad, but I admire her for embracing her hair loss, especially when I have mine still tucked under my hat. Next thing, Linsey comes out and calls us through, telling me how incredibly well I look. All sat with our masks on and no shaking hands, the consultant asks what we understand to date. He soon goes into explaining the surgery and the extent of what is involved. 'This is major surgery and not without its risks and potential complications that we won't be aware of until we get in and see'. He then goes on to explain that the ultimate aim is to get 100% removal of the cancer, but that can only be done using the naked eye and that they cannot account for microscopic cells that may be left behind. Then he moves on to option B: delaying surgery until I've had my three more cycles of chemo, with the hope that both the markers will have reduced, and the tumour will hopefully have shrunk further. For me, the potential outcome will not be any different if they leave it another three months, as they will still not be able to guarantee 100% removal.

I talk it through with Andy and he agrees completely with my decision to just get on with it as soon as possible, and I feel everyone agrees with us too. I can see they were actually expecting me to say that, as I've just noticed the consent form right next to me on his desk anyway. That's all done then. The plan is to have me in on 12th June where my surgery will be done by Miss San, so I'm delighted. When Linsey takes us for a further chat, we bump into Miss San and she is so cheerful, saying she will see me in just over a week and not to worry as I will be fine.

We go to the quiet room and have a chat with Linsey, who asks if we have any questions. She reassures me that no questions are stupid, as this is something very new to us both and the last thing she wants is for us to go home and worry unnecessarily. We cover the pre-op and initial post-op recovery, where I will have a PCA (patient-controlled analgesia) pump and have a catheter in situ, and then the expected twelve-week recovery plan of Dos and Don'ts. She reminds us both that they are always at the end of the phone if we have any questions or concerns.

Having previously mentioned genetic testing at my initial appointment in February and being given all the relevant reading materials on it, she revisits my thoughts on this. It's a huge decision as it can have knock-on implications for my immediate family, but I think it would be better to know if I have a gene that they could also be carrying. Then they can act on it rather than not knowing and worrying. My taking the test does not automatically mean they will have to take a test themselves if mine is positive, but they will be able to access counselling and consider whether to have a test.

I agree to have it done, along with my other pre-op bloods, so Andy is asked to take a seat back in the waiting area and I get called through to the HCA to have these taken. The HCA has said that for the rest of the day I need to avoid using the arm the blood was taken from. So I said, 'Oh good, do you want to tell my husband that and he will have to get tea tonight?'. She laughs and as she opens the door, she calls him over. With a very deadpan face she says, 'She mustn't use this arm at all tonight, as I've had difficulty getting blood today. So you will have to get tea'. She is so convincing as Andy agrees, with such a serious face, and then says, 'Nothing new there then, duck' and laughs.

I think we are both feeling so relieved that it's going ahead, with not too long to wait now. It's going to be a big thing having major surgery and having to go it alone, with no permitted visitors and Andy not even able to walk me to the ward on the day of the surgery. But again, I'm not on my own, as every person in the hospital is also being denied visitors for the safety and well-being of all staff and patients alike.

Making sure I've let my closest know the plan, I give Aunty Pam a ring to let her know what they've said, as she has also been told she is at a point now where she too will be having this surgery very soon. It's so good that we can at least support each other through the ups and downs of this nightmare journey. I can't say how much I wish things were very different though. I explained the discussions around the pros and cons of the surgery for me, but obviously we are all different, so I reiterate how important it is for her to make her own decisions. I know we're of a similar mindset, but she will now go to her appointment on Monday better informed and perhaps prepared with her own set of questions before making this big decision for her.

Only a week to go now before my 'big op', or as my late mother, having worked at the Royal Hallamshire Hospital Jessop Wing in Yorkshire, would tell me her ladies would say, 'I'm having *the major*, or 'I'm having it all *tooke*'. Aunty Pam has rung me today to say she was taken into hospital last night with what they suspect is a bowel obstruction and they have said it may be that her cancer has spread. I can't quite process this, as only a few days ago her team were looking to schedule her in for surgery too, so what has changed so drastically?

Inside I'm so worried about her and pray that it's nothing more than her issues with constipation. She has a pending appointment with the gynaecology surgeons in a couple of days, which was initially intended to discuss her proposed surgery. I know I can't do a huge amount practically, but I've got everything crossed for her as I remind her that I'm here at any time of the day or night and to please ring me if either she or Brian need anything at all. I understand how crushing and emotionally exhausting for everyone these so-called 'setbacks' are, and you don't feel like talking or texting anyone. So, I'll wait patiently for her to contact me.

Today's my pre-admission assessment appointment and I'm not worried in the slightest about the assessment, it's only if they come across a reason to have to cancel me. As I get called through, the practitioner is really pleasant. I take a seat and he asks me if I used to work on trauma orthopaedics at the hospital. Despite me feeling totally unrecognisable to those who know me, with my hat and mask on, no eyelashes or eyebrows, he still knew me, though I'm sure by name only. He used to be a theatre practitioner 'back in the day'. We have a good chat, reminisce and reflect on the 'good times'.

With what feels like a thorough MOT now complete, he goes through what I can expect post-op, leaving me with very little left to ask. It feels strange, but despite being informed of the potential risks, I, yes me and not my patient this time, will face, I'm not overly worried. You would think, being on the receiving end, hearing the risks associated with this specific surgery, including possible haemorrhage, development of clots and/or infection, pain, a bowel tear, or even ending up with a stoma, that I would be nervous, but I can't be. This option has been offered by professionals who have mutually agreed that this would be in my best interest, and my accepting their offer means that I will have a greater chance of a longer survival from this cancer. I really can't wait for my body to be rid of this 'unwelcome, unpredictable, life-destroying mass' that's sitting inside of me.

I can't get Aunty Pam out of my mind, so when I get back I message her to see how her appointment went. Her response was the last thing I could have truly imagined, giving me a heavy, sickening feeling in my tummy. She texts that ‘it has not been good news’ and that ‘she needs time to digest it’. I don’t want to push anymore, so I send her all our love and hugs and again give them the time they need right now. Knowing Pam, I think she will maintain radio silence until after my operation, to allow me time to recover and start to heal, without worrying me more. What a horrendous and devastatingly emotional situation we have found ourselves in.

It’s the day before my operation and I’ve been getting loads of messages wishing me good luck. Yesterday my friend Kim Facetimed me, which was so nice. I was talking about the associated risks of the surgery and my fear of possibly needing a permanent stoma formed. Her reply, as always, was spot on: ‘Yeh, and you will still be alive though!’ as she pointed at herself as an example of overcoming adversity. We had a great giggle and a bit of our usual ‘top-trumping’ regarding our conditions, our bit of mutual humour that we share to help manage our experience of illness.

Before she goes, she wishes me good luck and then the words, ‘See you on the other side’ spill out. Well, we both laugh until we cry. ‘Thanks Kim, that’s just what I want to hear just before I go for major surgery'. I knew exactly what she had meant to say, but with her dysphasia (speech impairment) following her stroke three years prior, it didn't come out as hoped. I said, 'I'm hoping you meant "see you after your operation"?' She's still laughing, nods and says 'YES'.

# Chapter 11

# 'The Major'

That's the early breakfast done and I'm now officially starving. I feel a bit nervous, albeit strangely, with a hint of excitement too. My head is mixed with so many thoughts and emotions right now. Double-checking my bag once again to make sure I've not missed anything; a lovely shower and I just want to put a photo and message for Andy to find under his pillow tonight. When we get to the hospital, it feels so clinical as Andy can't come in and has to say goodbye in the car. We are both a bit emotional but trying our best not to fully reveal how we're feeling. He gets my bags out of the car as I put my face mask on and all alone, I head into the hospital, turning around to see Andy looking so helpless, worried, and equally as alone.

On the day ward I'm soon admitted, with various doctors, including Miss San and the anaesthetist, coming to see me over the next few hours. It's actually happening, as Miss San takes my hand and promises to personally ring Andy after my operation to tell him how everything went. This is great for both of us, with him not being able to come in to see me or speak to me initially post-op, so I give him a quick call to let him know. For now, I try to distract myself with my iPad, but it doesn't really work for long. It doesn't exactly help with me being a 'nosey nurse' either.

It's now 13:00 and the nurse comes to ask me to get changed into my gowns. She's about to say how to put them on, but soon realises I'm already well-versed in putting gowns on and says, 'I expect you've done this once or twice before?' as she smiles and closes my curtains around the bed space. On her return, armed with my file, she's escorted by a Theatre porter and another nurse. With Theatre only across the corridor, we're soon there, as I pass a group of health professionals in their scrubs and masks all talking outside the door. I'm taken round the corner and handed over by my nurse to the Theatre nurses.

I'm quite concerned now. Why are all those people gathered outside the Theatre doors? Is my operation unusual? Are they all coming in to observe, and why? Why haven't I been asked if they can observe? As I'm asked if I can walk across into the Anaesthetic Room, I have to ask my questions. The nurse soon assures me that they had simply congregated there, but were definitely not involved in my case at all, and offered an apology for my understandable concern.

Once in the anaesthetic room I'm greeted by a very cheerful and witty anaesthetist. He explains what he's going to do and exactly what to expect when I wake in Recovery. My main question is the PCA. 'Oh yes, that will be up and it's going to be your best friend for a few days now'. Well, that was a great start. Next I'm having some boots put on!! They are Flowtron boots, used to help in the prevention of blood clots during and after major surgery. They're not turned on at this point, so I'm yet to have the whole experience. Still very self-conscious about my hair loss with strangers, I ask the nurse if she can ensure I have my hat put back on when I'm in recovery, and she promises I will. Next, I'm cannulated, ready for my anaesthetic medications. The anaesthetist explains that he's going to put an oxygen face mask over me now and just give me some oxygen first, before the medications. He says the medications will feel like a nice glass of gin, or two, as I laugh, saying, 'I'll have the two please'.

I seem to have someone telling me, 'You've had your operation, Julia, it's all done now'. The voice tells me I have my pain control pump, my PCA, as she places it in my hand and tells me to use it whenever I feel any pain coming on, and to tell her if it's not taking the pain away. I had half expected to be in a lot of pain when I came round, but I can't actually say I am. 'You also have your catheter in, Julia, so just relax and don't worry about needing the toilet.' As she tells me she will be staying right with me until I return to the ward, I try to focus on this reassuring, blurry figure in scrubs sat beside me and simply say, 'Thank you.' My legs feel so strange and I can't quite process why. I assume she must be checking my blood pressure on my thigh, but in fact it was my Flowtron boots inflating and deflating. I can hear people talking to me, but I just can't wake up enough to answer back right now. I remember asking my nurse if I have my hat back on and she reassures me I have. I just feel better knowing I'm not laid there with my bald but spikey head on full view. It's funny how I can barely stay awake, yet I can still think about things like this.

I think I may have been in recovery for a few hours, I'm not sure, but the next thing I am aware of is my recovery nurse telling me she is getting everything ready to take me back to the ward. I'm now more able to focus on her and engage in what I hope is a little bit of sensible conversation as she sorts me out ready for my transfer. I'm moved into a bay with three other ladies, who I've never met before, as I'm now back on the Gynaecology Ward, in the same bay I was in back in February. I try to say hello, in a woozy kind of fashion, and get a lovely welcome from them all. The rest of the day is spent having my obs done, my boots inflating and deflating, and me happily pressing my PCA, remembering what I was told by Paul in PreAMS.

Well, it's been a night of infusion alarms and changes, PCA pressing and obs... oh, and of course, Flowtron boots doing their stuff. Saying that, I think I slept reasonably well in between. I can focus better on my 'neighbours' this morning as we all start the day, and it's lovely that they all seem concerned as to how I'm feeling. I really need to sit up for breakfast, but

I'm dreading the thought of moving. I last pressed my pump about 10 minutes ago and in just shuffling my bottom a bit, along with having the boots on, it's quite uncomfortable, to be honest, so I give it another press.

I'm feeling so self-conscious, worrying that the staff may know I'm a nurse. I have no idea if they do, but whilst that mutual respect and understanding is nice, it can leave you feeling inadvertently anxious, like you need to behave as a 'perfect patient'. I know it would have no bearing on my care and recovery anyway, but just in case, I try my hardest not to cause them any extra work. Like most nurses, finding yourself on the other side isn't easy, as you don't want to be seen as a wimp either, but I've never personally had major abdominal surgery before and there is no standard textbook to follow for patients.

A lovely HCA asks if I want to sit up a little and, unsure of what she was expecting me to be able to do, I ask if she would help me. She seems to fully understand and draws the curtains round. As I psych myself up and take her offered arm, we both notice how swollen my left hand and forearm are. My PCA cannula is in the back of this hand but has clearly tissued (the cannula has come out of the vein and is leaking into the tissues), which means I won't have been getting my pain relief as prescribed. I still need to move, but feel as if my wound is going to burst open if I move anymore. But I know I must keep going, else I'm going to be there all day. The pain is pretty scary, but she assures me I can do it and I do.

A staff nurse comes to me and soon my PCA is turned off and the cannula removed. I can just manage to move my wedding ring but I think I'll take it off for now, just in case it gets tighter, as I'd hate to have to have it cut off. Because I'm now without my pain relief I'm a little anxious, but fortunately I'm quite easy to cannulate and it's not too long before I have a new cannula put in and my pump is set up again. Today, I've got to spend the day in bed, which I'm actually quite happy about. So before I have my assisted wash in bed, I have my boots removed for good and it feels so liberating. It's almost like taking your bra off at the end of the day. It's so lovely to have a wash – of a fashion, fresh bedding, a lovely cool strappy nightie on and to be able to clean my teeth.

One of the gynaecology consultants has come to see me on his daily ward round. He's very keen to pass on a message from Miss San to say how incredibly well the surgery had gone and how pleased she was with everything. He also tells me she rang Andy last night to tell him the same. It's so reassuring to hear how pleased she was with the surgery and as I lie here, with time to think about all that's happening to me, I sense this is far better than what they'd hoped to achieve.

Each morning my priority is to let Andy and Ross know how I am and what's happening with me. They are the most important people to let know and to hear everything first-hand. Andy and I Facetime on and off through the day and I'm having loads of text messages as well. Wherever possible, I text or ring family and friends as well to keep them all posted. I've spent most of the afternoon sleeping on and off. I think it's the pain relief being absorbed after leaking into my tissues and with my working pump too, I'm hardly surprised I'm sleeping so much! Well, I certainly don't have pain now anyway.

I think I lay awake for much of the night. You hear every noise, no matter how little. Poor Linda, across from me, has had a particularly bad night. I gave her the occasional wave in the dimmed lights, just so she could feel she wasn't alone. I couldn't really do an awful lot from my bed, but the nights can be so long and I knew how upset she was.

The ‘team’ are here and it looks like I’m getting out of bed... with help. This is quite a daunting prospect, but it’s all progress and I really hope these staples are up to the job. Tentatively, I manage to get to the side of the bed, as my HCA takes care of my catheter and drip stand for me. No rush, but I’m soon on my feet and cautiously stepping round to my chair. I’ve surprised myself and feel so happy to be out of bed, as all the ladies give me a little clap, asking how I feel.

It's a wash sat in my chair as I manage to do most things, apart from my back and legs myself. The anti-embolus socks are far too great a challenge for now and, I imagine, probably for the next week, but my HCA kindly does the honours for me. When I’m all done and feeling ‘great’, the staff nurse comes to remove my wound dressing. I’m fascinated as I have a good look at it, with my tummy still very swollen and misshapen and a wound curving round my belly button, down to my bikini line. Not ever having any surgical scars before, I’m thinking this is one hell of a scar! It looks a bit like a small mountain range with a cycle path running through the middle, but you know, I’m not bothered by it as, at the end of the day, it's only a scar and every scar tells a story. Mine is a story of survival.

The comradery amongst us, in these challenging times, is wonderful. We are all trying to be the replacement support of family and friends that none of us can have right now, but clearly and understandably feel in need of. Now I'm more mobile, I'm soon joining in the giving of any support we can offer right now. For each of us, these are long days, with times of personal emotional vulnerability. With having to go through your day with no visitors, due to the current restrictions, it's so reassuring and a comfort to have such lovely people to talk and listen to.

We share our stories, offer a sympathetic listening ear, swap magazines, and lovely Linda even brings goodies back for us all from the shop. It's interesting how people's paths cross and the benefits you get from meeting a complete stranger at a time of such vulnerability. The four of us all have our own stories to tell. I've been chatting to the one lady who has just had the same surgery as me, and she's doing really well. Linda, opposite me, is having a tough time with her pain. I think she looks to me a bit like a mother figure. Although I can't and wouldn't give medical advice, I find myself offering basic advice and a listening ear when she seems to need one. At the end of the day I care, and I think people sense that. I'm sure, at times, I have a big sign on my head saying, *Talk to me, I'm a nurse*.

I'm not feeling great this evening. I don't know if I've overdone things. I just want to lie down and be quiet for a bit. Earphones in, music on and I manage to get a few naps. The nurse came earlier to empty my catheter leg bag, but I've just woken feeling like I need to pass urine. I'm getting horrible spasmodic and wind pains in my tummy. My catheter bag had filled to full in a matter of a few hours and I think some of the pain is from the back pressure it's caused. It turns out my temperature is also raised now. I feel like I've taken several steps back in my recovery, and I'm really worried something has gone wrong and I might have a brewing infection. The pains are not easing despite using my PCA, but they say they can't give me anything else other than the paracetamol, which seem to make no difference. The nurse has asked the doctor to review me, but he's currently busy. In the interim, they all remain very attentive as they can see how distressed I am.

It was after midnight before the doctor was able to get to see me. He knelt beside my bed and seemed genuinely concerned. As we discussed the pains, he said, 'You're a nurse, right?' Smiling, I said, 'I'm afraid so' and ask if I could try Buscopan and perhaps some peppermint water, which he was apparently about to suggest anyway. I think my pain eventually started to ease by about 02:30. That was the last time I remember looking at the clock anyway.

The following morning, Miss San walks in and looks at me, with her beaming smile and says, 'You look great, how are you feeling?'. 'Apart from last night's 'blip', I'm feeling good, thank you'. Reiterating how pleased she was with my operation, she goes into a lot of detail as to what she found and carefully removed. With everything she's done, I can only feel extremely lucky and thankful that I was offered the operation when I was, especially as I'd had suspicious deposits on the lining of my bowel too. 'It really couldn't have gone any better', she says as she takes a look at my wound and reassures me that the abdominal swelling will eventually settle.

As I give Andy, Ross and Nic my morning 'Facetime update', I feel so lifted today. They're so encouraging and positive. The gynae team are all truly fabulous and I feel so safe and comforted by Miss San's optimism. The outcome of the surgery has reinforced my determination to keep looking forward and show everyone how strong and grateful I am for everything.

Well, a disturbed night for everyone, I think, as Mother Nature excelled herself. We had an unbelievable thunder and lightning storm which at one point felt like it shook the whole building. Apart from the mounting sleep deprivation, I feel pretty good. Desperate to convince Miss San I'm well enough to go home, I walk past the desk where she is talking. She says, 'Good morning, you look so well, you look more like a visitor. I expect you're wanting to go home?' Yes, it's worked, I think to myself, as I quickly reply, 'Oh yes'. She smiles and says, 'Just one more day, I really don't want you to have any setbacks for the sake of just one more day'. Whilst I'm a bit disappointed, I do understand. My body and my mind have been through such a lot and I don't want to undo everything I've achieved to date, especially when there's still such a long road ahead.

Another early morning shower and I've already managed to pack much of my case in anticipation. And it's a 'Yes', I'm going home!! Linsey, my gynaecology CNS, comes to see me, amazed at how well I'm looking. She recalls how poorly I was in the earlier days at diagnosis and now, after major surgery, I look so well. It's another lovely boost to my morale right now. Soon my gift bag of medications, sharps box and injections, spare dressings and clip removers arrives, and with my 'chauffeur' waiting outside of the ward, I'm slowly walked to the doors of the ward, having declined the offer of a wheelchair.

# Chapter 12

# Healing

Apart from becoming reliant on an-all singing, all-dancing hospital bed that did everything to make life easier, especially after major abdominal surgery and then returning home to the reality of the challenges of a standard king-sized divan bed, my recovery period was pretty much as I had expected, and I was determined not to compromise it in any way.

My mood was positive, and I was determined not to let any negativity take hold. Together, Andy and I would sit and enjoy the garden and its views, rest whenever we needed to and value the regular visits at the lounge window, until we were finally allowed to socially distance in the garden with close family.

It's Nic's birthday and they both come round and join us in the garden for a while, which is lovely. We chat about life once this precious 'little lady' is born, and the feelings they are going to experience as parents. I can't wait to be a part of this next chapter in their lives and I'm so grateful I'm going to be over much of this treatment by then. It's days like these that are truly helping towards my healing process.

Dr Joe rings shortly after lunch for my telephone consultation and asks how I'm getting on since my surgery, sounding very pleased to hear how well it had gone. Apparently, my latest cancer markers have come down to 123 now, which is absolutely incredible. My heart is bursting with happiness... and he then says my liver function bloods (LFTs) are abnormal and he's not sure why! My heart has just crashed to the floor. I ask if it's anything to be worried about and he says he's not sure, but given the initial concern around my liver on the first scan in January, he wants me to have an abdominal scan to check. 'It may possibly be the chemo,' he says, 'but we will review your bloods again before your next chemo on 8th July and see what they're doing first.'

I was so happy about my markers, but now I can't stop worrying that there may be something serious going on with my liver. I can't help but wonder if it's secondary cancer and no matter how much everyone's trying to reassure me right now, my head won't stop mulling over his inability to totally reassure me. Being a nurse does have a downside when it comes to knowing so much about how the body can go wrong, especially when you work in a field such as palliative care! But right from the start, I told myself I'm going to have to switch my 'palliative nurse head' off and acknowledge that there are many positive stories that come from cancer journeys. The trouble with me is that I can give advice, but I'm not always the best at taking it. I can be so stubborn sometimes... 'a typical Taurean', they tell me.

So eventually, I give myself a good talking to and focus myself on a nice weekend, switching off from the 'C word', especially as it's taking up too much of my time just lately. We're on a mission today. Andy's just come back from having his first 'professional' haircut in nearly five months and tells me Chris has been laughing at my attempts to cut his hair through lockdown. As it was, no one had any choice at that time, so it was either that or to look like a hippie. At least I didn't cut round a pudding basin!

Ross and Nic pop round late afternoon. I think they must have heard we have ice creams! We would often have an evening of food and playing cards, but our 'visitor, Covid, is putting a stop to that at the moment. Never mind, I will still be up for thrashing them, as usual, when we next get the chance. Thinking about it, it might be quite a while with our beautiful baby granddaughter due in September. One thing is for sure, being born into this family, she will definitely grow up knowing how to play cards.

I've sent Andy out on his bike today. It really helps him and without this sounding uncaring, it helps me too. I need him to do all the things he enjoys and benefits from and equally, I need my space and my time for me. He's going to be returning to work tomorrow, having been furloughed for a long time, so it's going to be just me and Trigger and I'm actually quite excited about being left to look after myself.

Before I know it, Andy's day is done and he's taking me to the doctor's surgery for my pre-chemo bloods. We sit in the car park until the nurse comes out and calls me in. It all feels so strange, as the only people in the building are staff. The nurse reassuringly explains about all the cleaning and precautions they are following at the moment. They are having to allow so much longer for appointments, so it's lovely that she has time to chat and ask how I am getting on as well.

Delighted to know that Sue is in surgery today, I'm invited into her consulting room. 'Come on in chick, I've disinfected everything, including your chair'. It's so lovely to see her. The last time I saw her was in January, when she invited us in to receive my initial blood results. She's remained an ongoing support to both Andy and myself, either by phone or text, which has been deeply appreciated. She obviously has an awareness of everything I've been through to date, as she asks too about Andy and Ross and Nic and how the pregnancy is going. She has known me for so long now, seeing Ross grow up, and has always shown an interest and concern as to how he is.

Today's my fifth chemo, my first one since surgery. It's still early days as far as my recovery goes, but I must restart my chemo now so as not to disrupt my treatment plan. The chemo will hopefully help to mop up any cancer cells that might be floating around from my surgery. The first thing I'm desperate to know is how my bloods are since my operation. Becky smiles and informs me my Ca 125 has dropped to 14. 'Sorry, what did you say it was?' I had heard right... 14. In six months, my cancer markers had gone from 4,274 down to 14! My liver function was also apparently showing signs of a gradual improvement. My 'happy tears' start to flow as I try not to overthink what this could mean in the long term. I desperately need a massive cuddle right now, but for now I'm content with the relief I'm feeling. I ring Andy and Ross to let them know and unsurprisingly, they're elated. I work my way through everyone I need to let know and the reactions are heart-warming.

All the pain and heartache to date has reaped its rewards for me and I'm so grateful for everyone who has enabled me to reach this point. People presume it must be awful having to spend a whole day on a chemo unit having 'poison' pumped into your veins. Well, I could think of better ways of spending my days, but for me, it was mind over matter.

Clair pops in to see me and can't get over how well I look, so soon after surgery. She's very pleased with my markers and feeling confident that the LFTs are more likely to be the liver trying to cope with the effects of the chemo, and the fact that they are slowly improving means she feels it's unlikely to be anything to worry about. I've asked about what the plan will be after my last cycle of chemo next month. 'You will go onto a maintenance treatment plan which will be 18 treatments in total, including the ones you've already had.' This is the Avastin target therapy that I've had with some, but not all, of my chemo treatments. It will be every three weeks, as an infusion on the CTU. I will probably be in no longer than two hours in total; I can cope with that.

Another week into my recovery and apart from the usual post-chemo days, I'm feeling pretty good. Linsey has just rung to tell me some fantastic news. Initially reassuring me it's absolutely nothing to worry about, she goes on to say that my genetic test results were back and my BRCA test was negative. I can't describe how relieved I feel. This is about my family and their future health. To think that you could be carrying a gene that may also devastate the life of someone you love, is too difficult and painful to imagine. I'm straight on the phone to Ross first and then everyone else in my immediate family, to take that worry away from them right now.

Whilst my latest bloods are slowly coming down, they remain deranged. Dr Joe still wants me to have the abdominal ultrasound to check my liver out, along with repeat bloods. So that's my heart pounding through my chest once again. He tells me he will ring me next Friday with all the results. We talked about life after chemo and the maintenance therapy Clara had talked about. We also touched on returning to work... something I never thought I would be able to do. He certainly doesn't rule it out but is keen for me to complete my treatment first.

Another quick appointment through, this time for my ultrasound. My sonographer is another familiar face from previous appointments. He's lovely as always and clearly remembers me from before. He chuckles as I say I think I'm probably seeing him and his team more than my friends just lately. I take my place up on the couch as the lights go down. The 'nice cold jelly' goes on and he starts orientating himself around my abdomen. 'Okay, deep breath in for me and now push your tummy right out. Now onto your left side, breathe in and hold and breathe away'. We both start to laugh as he leans over to see my face and asks, 'Are you breathing?'

The constant stopping and clicking the keyboard always unsettles me, as I'm never really sure if that means they've found something or if it's just standard measuring of organs etc. Before I leave the room, he kindly reassures me he cannot see anything to be concerned about. He says he's had a really good look at the liver capsule and cannot see anything worrying. I am so relieved and thank him so much for telling me, which means I don't have another difficult few days waiting for my consultant to give me this news. My relief is massive, I can't tell you. I get back to the car and just break down. I need a bit of time to myself right now, time to fully process each and every word he said, to make sure I did hear correctly. When I'm ready I pop and see Andy down the road, at work. He's over the moon. On my way home I make my calls and send my text messages to everyone who's waiting to hear from me.

I pop round to see my best friend. It's the first time I've had the opportunity to do this since January and I really can't wait to see her and tell her my latest news. We sit in the garden and have some wonderful, much-needed time together. The garden is looking beautiful as we have a little stroll round and just embrace the moment. I think we are both feeling pretty emotional.

Today, Andy and myself are off to meet Baz. Apparently, he is the man to see for a natural wig and he doesn't disappoint. What a nice guy.

He apparently had leukaemia as a child and his parents were told he would not reach his 7$^{th}$ birthday, and I guess he's now around his late 50s. At the start of his career in hairdressing, he vowed he would especially concentrate on helping cancer patients with their hair and wigs. It's not long at all before I make my choice and he tells me I should give it a name. 'Ashley', I think, because of 'her' ash colours. I love her. She's nothing like my actual hair, but she will be fun to wear and I can change her style whenever I want to.

The weather has been lovely, so we both head over to the local garden centre for a wander round. We did well considering we weren't actually going for anything, instead coming away with a boot full of plants and several bags of compost, along with an enthusiastic me wanting them planting as soon as we get back. It was so lovely to be able to just wander around and take everything in, albeit with our masks on and socially distanced from all the gardening enthusiasts. We even took advantage of the ice cream van parked up on the common on the way back. Masks definitely off as we sit in the car with our 99s and enjoy our moment of pleasure and freedom.

# Chapter 13

# Looking to the Future

The past few days have been good and as promised, Dr Joe calls to tell me the scan results are back and my liver is normal. Although I had been told this before, it was lovely to have it confirmed after consultants had also reviewed. Whilst I had him on the phone, I thought I would take the opportunity to hear his thoughts on me considering working again. I've been pondering on the possibility of returning to the hospice, but I'm unsure if I am up to hands-on nursing again, especially in palliative care. He is clearly keen to encourage me to give this some serious thought, but only once my chemo is finished, especially in this time of a global pandemic and whilst immunocompromised. He goes on to explain about my ongoing target therapy up until June next year and how that should not hinder me working.

Having already made an appointment to speak with my first line manager to talk through my concerns and establish my options, I make my way to the hospice. It's the first time I've been in the hospice since I spoke with the staff when I was diagnosed, so it feels quite uncomfortable. On top of that, I still can't quite believe that I am thinking of returning to work, something I really didn't expect to happen, having been given a Stage 4 diagnosis. I am so proud of myself for even getting this far.

I'm worrying about not being able to offer the same level of care to my patients and their carers, and how that would ultimately impact both them and myself. I hold my hand up and say I am a perfectionist, as I feel a lot of us at the hospice are, so giving 110% is something I could certainly not compromise on. Palliative care is a wonderful yet emotionally draining field of practice and I know in my own mind, with my emotions having already taken such a battering, and with much more yet to come, I cannot risk compromising my health anymore. It would be like pressing the self-destruct button and expecting my family and close friends to deal with the aftermath, on top of everything else they are also trying to cope with.

I've accepted that, whilst I can't know if I could do this until I'd put my uniform back on and try it out, the thought of that alone makes me feel so anxious. I don't think I'm going to be able to take on my patients' and their carers' journeys and all that comes with that, whilst also trying to manage my own ongoing experience. So, with a heavy heart, I don't feel I have a choice. What this journey has taught me is that I must ensure I put myself first. I need to be compassionate toward myself for a change and give myself permission to do what's right for me.

So, I was quite honest about my concerns and asked about what alternative roles would be an option for me to consider if I was not able to cope with my role anymore. I knew I was a well-liked and valued member of the team who still had invaluable knowledge, skills and experience that the hospice could benefit from, but to cut a long story short, there were no options for me – it was my old job or nothing!! The offer followed: a phased return with me being supernumerary for a period to be agreed. They obviously weren't listening to what I was saying I needed. I felt the decision had clearly been made long before I'd even asked to make the appointment, and I certainly wasn't prepared to agree to a decision that would potentially break me, especially given everything I had been through to get to this point.

All I can say is I felt so unappreciated and unsupported; I was no more than a number after all these years of loyal service. I was hurt, more than I was prepared to let on, and with my emotions so close to the surface, it was difficult. But I was telling myself, 'This is nothing, nothing in comparison to what I've had to endure in order to get to this point and I'm certainly not prepared to let this break me again'. I agreed to a return to work on an induction programme, where I could complete mandatory and electronic learning courses, whilst also using some of my outstanding annual leave. This would give me time to consider my options and reach a decision.

Having not worked since January, we had the added stress of financial worry. I'd not received any guidance from work, other than a letter to advise me that I would not be paid from the end date of contractual sick pay. Thankfully, Linsey had given me information on MacMillan Cancer Support; they were amazing. I apparently qualified for Employment and Support Allowance (ESA) which was by no means on par with my salary, but it did offer us some financial comfort in the months ahead. We didn't want to unnecessarily worry family about any of this, so chose not to discuss it with them.

We were immensely grateful and deeply touched when my sister made a totally unexpected gesture of transferring a payment directly into our account to ensure we did not have the additional burden of financial worries in the uncertain days ahead. I can't tell you the difference her act of kindness has meant to us both.

It was only a matter of days into my induction and with Covid still rife, it was inevitable that at some point the hospice would find itself in its clutches and as anticipated it hit, resulting in me, to be safe, being furloughed until further notice. Back to social isolation once again, but this time worrying about my options for continuing to work at the hospice.

Determined not to allow all my worries to drag me down, I've accepted a very welcome invitation to catch up with two wonderful friends. I'm meeting up with Kim and Rachel at Kim's house. We are going to sit in the garden where we can all safely follow the distancing guidelines, drink tea and eat cake. I worked with Kim and Rachel for a number of years at the hospice; those were great times. Since then, both Kim and Rachel have also faced adversity, dealing with their own extremely challenging health problems whilst showing such courage and determination. So it was just lovely to be sat with these incredibly strong and inspiring women, my heroes for so many reasons.

I've bought the mandatory boxes of cakes and the brews are underway. We're soon catching up, and what stands out is how open and honest we are with each other about what we've either already been through or are still going through. Many people who have gone through a life-changing experience generally find their own ways of coping with their feelings and for some, there are going to be times when that element of what some might refer to as black humour creeps in. This was very much the case for Kim and myself, particularly as we chose to try and desensitise the seriousness of our recent life-changing experiences.

It is impossible to prepare for every situation that may arise along our life's path, as each one will often come with its own new, unique and challenging baggage. It is, however, important that we allow ourselves to just stop for a minute and acknowledge that our lives don't come with a standard user manual and as such, we will all be different in how we choose to cope day-to-day, sometimes hour-by-hour, and that's OK.

I don't know if Rachel has explored this coping strategy before, but I felt she really enjoyed giving it a go. Now for one of Kim's dysphasic *faux pas*. She was asking about my hair loss, so I whipped 'Ashley' off and they both said I looked great without hair. Kim was asking what colour I thought it would grow back. 'It's going to be a surprise,' I said. She then said, 'You want to die... NO, NOT AGAIN!' We can't stop laughing, as I knowingly ask, 'Did you mean DYE, I could always dye it?' She nods and we continue to laugh at her unfortunate remarks. I love how we can just laugh about these kinds of things together; it's so liberating.

Well, today's my last chemo session and a huge milestone for me. I'll still have to continue with my maintenance infusions every three weeks until June next year, so I will still be closely monitored. It feels like everything I've been through so far has reaped its reward and I have a big part of my life back again. My nurse and I get talking about whether I have any plans once I finish my chemo, and I tell her we really want a short break away somewhere in the UK. After having our lives pretty much put on hold since January, with me being in and out of hospital so much, having my chemo and having been socially isolated through shielding, we're both very much in need of a break. With Covid and restrictions changing daily, it's not going to be that easy to plan, so we'll probably have to consider a short-notice booking and see how we get on. Despite today being such a milestone, it feels a bit of an anti-climax, to be honest. Maybe it's just me – whilst I am so relieved it's all done now, I'd just thought there may have been some recognition of what today has meant for me. Not even a ringing of a bell on the unit, it's been just another day.

I think I'm going to wear 'Ashley' and a bit of 'lippy' today. I might not be going out anywhere, but it does make me feel better. I'm going to do a bit more baking today: it's going to be a flapjack day, just to keep Andy happy. He says they're great for when he goes on his bike rides, which are usually alternate days, yet 'strangely', he still manages to get through rather a lot in a day, and they're usually all gone in two or three days.

My phone rings with a Facetime call from Lynn congratulating me on finishing my last chemo. 'I had to ring you, you can't put something like this in a text.' As someone who has personal experience of their own cancer journey, she just gets me right now. She knows, hurdle by hurdle, just what this whole journey is about and how marking these kinds of achievements is so important for someone going through gruelling cancer treatment. We're on the phone for about an hour all in all as we laugh, reflect and look to the future for us both and our families.

The past few days of post-chemo have been as challenging as usual, especially at night. I've been feeling so fatigued at the slightest bit of exertion, and very little sleep at night isn't really helping matters. Currently, we have a very uncomfortable and draining heatwave, with temperatures around 30 degrees Celsius in the day and unwelcome hot and very humid nights, allowing very little respite/rest. I don't think it's been this unbearable for a long time. There's no 'Ashley' or hat today as my head is sweating constantly, with the sweat dripping down in front of my ears and onto my neck. It's not the best look going, and I'm feeling really self-conscious with it. I'm constantly wiping my face and neck and mopping my head with a cool tea towel run under the cold tap, feeling like I'm about to faint. I really hope no one comes round today, otherwise I'm going to have to put my hat on for a while and 'melt' even more. I suppose that's one bonus to the weather: you don't need an excuse to have an extra ice cream if you want one.

Today is the official day my statutory sick pay (SSP) ends. I've had this for the 28 weeks now, so I'm going to have to wait to find out if I now qualify for benefits. I'm so angry about our situation now, as we are having to wait without money coming in, other than my pension, until my claim is processed. MacMillan Welfare had contacted me before and explained I could apply so many weeks before my SSP was due to end. Having never had to claim for benefits before, I wasn't aware my SSP ran alongside my employer's sick pay and therefore, it would finish four weeks earlier than I'd been expecting. If my employers had made me aware of this from the start, I would have been able to make my claim well enough in advance not to have a gap in money coming in. It really is just another worry you can do without whilst you have so much going on in your lives. You have so much to think about and process, which can be difficult enough anyway, when some days your head is a complete fog.

How different the days can be. A parcel has arrived today and I have absolutely no idea where it's come from. It's a lovely wicker hamper with jars of sweets, gin and tonic popcorn, a bottle of champagne and two champagne flutes. All I have to go on is a card saying 'Congratulations Julia'. Whoever it's from, it's perfectly timed as I've been feeling so down and sleep-deprived from the heat over the past few days. After a few discreet enquiries, I find out the mystery gift had come care of my sister and her husband, sent to mark me completing my chemo.

# Chapter 14

# Remission

Today's oncology phone call comes through much earlier than planned and that's got my heart pounding once again. With a quick reassurance that there is nothing bad to tell me, Dr Joe says he wants me to have a CT scan, as a 'baseline for the future'. It's strange how you feel when you're due to have a scan; your feelings are all over the place. You want to have a scan, but only on the proviso that you're going to be told everything is good. But now, there will forever be that underlying fear of it not being what we want to hear and nobody can offer any reassurance to ease the unrelenting anguish. The various, well-meaning platitudes will continue to come, offering kind and goodhearted words of reassurance, yet the uncertainty they carry will only serve to offer hope rather than promises.

With the scan done, the wait seems somehow worse. You know that now, someone has information about you and how that information is going to impact your future, yet you're having to wait to know what that is. You, like everyone else, are in an orderly queue whilst the emotional rollercoaster just keeps running.

I have been taking advantage of my freedom from chemo over the past few weeks, which has been so refreshing. Whilst my maintenance treatment is still ongoing, the appointments are significantly shorter and the aftereffects are far less disabling. Life 'almost' feels normal again. I have had an 'end of chemo afternoon tea' with Pam and the girls, whizzed round my friend's garden on her sit-down mower chased by her dog, participated and contributed to Nic's baby shower, had our first meal out in over 9 months and even had my eyebrows microbladed for the first time.

Once on chemo, you are unable to have microblading until you have completed all your treatment, so to be able to finally have a chance to have some eyebrows back, helping to frame my face, was so important for me. I have tried every single day to get dressed, put on some makeup and do what I can with my 'new look', despite how I was feeling, both inside and out.

To me, that was so important to keep doing regardless. Molly was so kind and totally understanding of what her treatments meant for people such as me, people with enforced hair loss, and her time and dedication to helping me in this transition was invaluable. Once she was ready to hand me the mirror to see my eyebrows stenciled on, I was so nervous, as I also desperately wanted to look as natural as possible. As I looked up, I found myself looking at an image that offered a resemblance to who I used to be – me before cancer took it all away – and it was just the best feeling in the world. Overcome with emotion, my tears once again took hold as I embraced this very small but precious part of my identity, albeit stenciled in place.

It's been a very long ten days since my CT scan, and with barely a wink of sleep between us and the house cleaned within an inch of its life, we are heading off for my scan results appointment at the hospital. It's that awful silence in the car again as we both contemplate what awaits us. The hospital remains unusually quiet, with many appointments continuing to be held remotely where possible. We're greeted by Lisa, who's an HCA in outpatients, and also Nic's godmother. She says she won't come into my consultation because of knowing me so well, and whilst I say I'm happy for her to be in there, she feels it wouldn't be right for me and reassures me that it's not because she knows anything, because she doesn't.

At that point Dr Joe opens his door, offering a gentle smile, and invites us to come in and sit down. My legs are like jelly and my heart is pounding so forcefully. After asking how we both are, he asks where 'things' are at the moment. The conversation continues for a few minutes as we recap the past few months. From there it leads him to mention my last CT results. He says, 'There's no cancer anymore, Julia, it's all gone. That's why you're looking and feeling so well'. As he leans forward, he keeps eye contact with me and smiles (well, his eyes are smiling anyway; I can't see beyond his mask, until he decides to lower it. 'You can't believe it, can you?'

In total shock, I'm struck dumb, the tears just keep flowing as I continue to look into his eyes, and I simply shake my head in disbelief. I look at Andy and he's really emotional too. It feels like there is only the three of us in the world right now with nothing else around us, just living that moment and not considering anything else at all. I can't believe I've gone from a Stage 4 cancer diagnosis to being told it's all gone! He gives us time before he continues to explain that he's gone over and over the scan pictures himself as he goes through the before and after images with us. He then shows us the reporting of my results which starts with *No evidence of disease present*.

I'm sure he doesn't get many opportunities to give such amazing news to people, and I can clearly see in his eyes how happy he is for us both. My cancer markers are 'normal' and he reassures me that the team will continue to monitor these. Whilst he can never make promises for the future, he says, 'The cancer may or may never come back again, and apart from the only two certainties we all have in life, as you well know, we cannot rely on anything else, so just go away now and live your life to the full; make sure you go and celebrate well and don't leave it for tomorrow or another day – do it today.' He continues, 'I can see the tears are happy tears, and so they should be. You have done so incredibly well.'

I mention about wanting to try to return to work soon, and he advises me that my immune system will probably take about six months to recover, so we must both remain Covid-aware and continue to follow all the safety guidelines in place. He wants me to try and avoid close contact with any known respiratory patients when I go back to work, and offers to write a supporting letter if I need one.

I ask about my bloods and mention my recent raised cholesterol levels. He smiles and says, 'Yes, I've seen this, but avoided mentioning it after giving you such wonderful news; I didn't want to spoil the moment.' I told him I've already been focusing on changing my diet recently and as we all smile, I tell him I think all this lockdown baking hasn't exactly helped.

'I'm just so, so grateful for everything you and your entire team have done for me. I really can't thank you enough. Please will you pass on my gratitude to each and every one of them for me?' As he gently nods his head in recognition, he acknowledges I'm right – it is very much a team effort, and he most certainly will let everyone know. As we stand, he's still smiling and says, 'I want to give you a hug, but we can't.' One day when Covid becomes a distant memory, I will hold him to that hug. As we come out, Lisa sees us and asks if we are both okay. My eyes are still full, but I'm able to reassure her they're happy tears. With a tear now in her eyes too, she offers a gestured hug to us both, before we set off to ring Ross.

The rest of my day has just been crazy with phone calls, going to see family, text messages back and to. We head out for our celebratory meal, just the two of us. Ross and Nic should be with us, but Nic's had to go to hospital for a midwifery check-up and we're not sure when or if she's coming home tonight. As I look around the restaurant, I think I'm seeing people in a completely different way. I really want to shout out my news and go to every table and say, 'Excuse me, can I tell you I've just been told today that I've beaten cancer?'. Instead, we quietly blend into the steady rumble of conversations and celebrations. The atmosphere is great, with music, surprise cakes, staff and customers clapping as the cakes get brought to the different tables. I just want to embrace it all. The meal and wine are really lovely, but it's not long before the emotional exhaustion starts to hit us both. So, with closing time earlier than usual anyway, thanks to the persistence of Covid, we head home for PJs and some quiet downtime.

Today is the first day of not having that awful cancer cloud hanging over us, and my head is still trying to process what I have been able to achieve. It's really hard to explain – your head is wanting to save that unbelievable high, thinking about every word you've just been told, but there is a persistent niggle that wants to spoil it for you, saying, 'Are you sure you heard it right? You were told you have a Stage 4 cancer diagnosis and now you're meant to be cancer-free?!! You've gone and told so many people now… I hope you're right; I hope he was right.'

It's only been three very emotional days since we were told I'm in remission and this morning, we have been further blessed with the news of the safe arrival into the world of our absolutely beautiful granddaughter Grace, assured that mum and baby are doing well! I can't tell you how emotional I feel seeing the pictures of Ross gently cradling her as Nic watches on with so much love and happiness in both their eyes. I've been given the chance to enjoy being a part of their life as a family, building wonderful memories together and just embracing a time I can now look forward to, watching Ross and Nichola become the most wonderful parents.

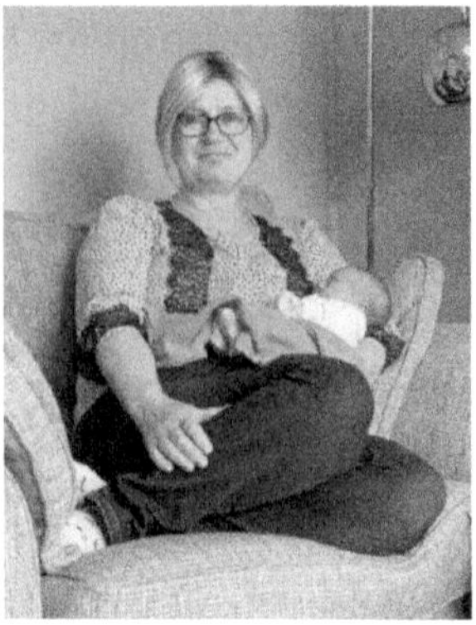

...

**My first cuddles as a Granny**

**Grace 2020**

It felt quite apt to choose this moment to end my diary. A time to keep looking forward and not ruminate too much on the past. Whilst I accepted that life would never quite be the same anymore, that life had been given back to me and I was determined to start enjoying it again, along with my wonderful family and friends. The diary proved a great filler of unwelcome times and created a safe place to store my thoughts and memories as I learnt to adjust to a life 'damaged' by cancer. As I closed my diary, I simply wrote, 'Goodbye cancer… your visit was never welcome here, your visit is never welcome anywhere.'

# Chapter 15

# We all have a Purpose in Life

With maintenance treatment still ongoing and chemo now out of the way, I was increasingly keen to look at what the future had to offer me, and more so, what I could offer it. I remained very passionate about my job, but knew that returning as a hands-on staff nurse was an unrealistic expectation, a realisation predominantly based on my emotional well-being rather than my physical well-being. I was not ready, not by any means, to give up on caring for others. I had experience, skills, knowledge, passion, and a determination to continue to fulfil my dream, but to personally manage that, I had to let go and sacrifice my privileged role of nearly 37 years.

Keen to look at the future and what I wanted to do with my life, I arranged a day to have a meeting with my first-line manager within the next few weeks, where I could talk through my options for returning to the hospice to work. I had already reached, in my own mind, the painful decision of not returning to nursing, but I knew I still had vast knowledge, experience and skills that could be utilised within the hospice. But little did I know that this was a decision that had already been made for me, regardless of what or how I felt.

Despite being very open and honest about my own worries as to whether I was to return to hands-on nursing again, it turned out my fears didn't count, or at least that was how it felt from this angle. It was going to have to be my old job or nothing, 'I'm afraid', regardless of the subsequent implications that would have for me. Regardless of my inner strength and determination to overcome this very painful journey and even consider choosing to continue working and helping those who came into our care, I was being given the option of compromising my well-being for the sake of filling a nursing position or being put out to graze whilst they replaced me.

I was not prepared to compromise my very precious health, something that so many people had worked so hard with me to get back, purely because it fitted with someone else's needs. The lack of consideration and compassion was certainly felt, and I needed to consider where I went from here. So I agreed to work through an initial 12-week Return to Work programme, where I would complete all my inhouse training and updates, whilst giving thought to my future.

Having only been back at the hospice for a matter of days, it was inevitable that, like so many other organisations, the hospice would be badly hit by the Covid outbreak, and I was soon told I needed to furlough until further notice. So once again, I was back at home and unable to work, but it did give me the time to think more about what I was going to do with my life.

I had also been keeping in close phone contact with Aunty Pam's partner, Brian. Pam had been quite quickly deteriorating, and I was now offering my palliative knowledge and experience to guide him through what was becoming increasingly evident as near to end of life care. My heart was breaking for them both, and all I could offer was advice and all my love. They lived too far away to be able to see them, but I totally respected that this was very much

Pam's time and she did not want visitors coming and going. She knew I was with her in my thoughts and prayers.

Having someone so close and dearly loved going through the same journey as you, but finding them approaching the terminal phase of their illness, was something I really struggled with. My initial markers had been significantly higher than Pam's, yet we had both gone through chemotherapy and were at the point of being considered for the same surgery one minute, and then the next minute she wasn't. She was so happy for me, but all I could think was how unfair and wrong it all seemed. I didn't even want to mention how well I was getting on; how could I? I was being given a chance of life and she had been told there were no options for her. Painfully, the day came when Pam lost her fight and we all lost a truly wonderful, kind and funny friend, the person I saw more as my second mum, and I will forever treasure her love and laughter and our shared memories.

Whilst everyone was getting excited for Christmas, having just come out of the second lockdown restrictions, we were dealing with yet another of the hardest months in our family's lives. Pam passed away on the fourth anniversary of my dear father's death, and within a matter of days the world lost another incredible person: Baz, AKA 'Beaut', who also left us way too soon, still with so much to do. My late mum's and grandfather's anniversaries were both on Christmas Day and so, as with every past Christmas Day, we toasted and took time to remember all those who were no longer with us.

2021 arrived and, despite my feeling emotionally exhausted, time moved on. But with us now into a third lockdown, I couldn't just meet up with friends and talk about how I was feeling and get a hug. It was like stepping back into March 2020. Again facing very difficult feelings, I worked through my days as before, trying to keep busy, with some 'normality', yet allowing myself to sit and reflect and let out some tears every now and again. That was all I could do – that was all anyone in my position could do.

It was now time to start thinking about work again and to try looking outside of the box. Ironically, I had actually begun this process some years previously as I knew there was a role to be filled, one that would prove invaluable to the hospice on several counts. Regrettably, while I was praised for bringing my ideas and presentation to the table, no one at that time had been willing to embrace my vision for change.

While still being furloughed from work, I had to now consider what to do with my nursing registration. My three-yearly revalidation was up for renewal in April, so I had to decide if I was going to relinquish it or keep myself available and on the register for now. I had invaluable knowledge and skills that could be used in other clinical setting, ones that would qualify me for other clinically based positions, clearly elsewhere. So my mind was made up, and I arranged an appointment at work to get my portfolio of required evidence signed off for another three years of practice. What happened next changed my life to this day.

After my appointment, I had a chance to meet and chat more with my new manager, Neil, who had very recently come into the post, only a few days before. The understanding, compassion and empathy I received at that time was life-changing for me. He was very keen to meet and listen to my predicament and to explore my wishes for the future, and offered his full respect for even considering working in the same setting, given all I had gone through. I couldn't believe that, after previously being firmly told I could only return as a practicing staff nurse, he too shared my vision for change and embraced my dedication. Despite only being in post for such a short time, he said he could already see how both my returning and developing a role of this nature would only serve to benefit the hospice and its service users going forward.

I believe this man saved me in terms of my own mental health at that time. I had fought so hard through some dark days of adversity to get to where I was, knowing I would face further hardship but still with the strength to show my worth. He recognised that, rather than casting me onto the 'unwanted' pile. He lifted me out of a downward spiral of depression that could quite easily have taken me with it.

The weeks following our meeting offered some fruitful conversations and meetings, structured around the foundations of my gently nurtured return to work. Having been asked what I wanted and how the organisation could help me, the role was very much tailored to my ongoing needs, offering me control and time to adjust, and in return I was offering my 100% commitment to the hospice.

As I settled back into a working pattern, I began to look at the groundwork needed to bring about my vision. As with implementing any change in the workplace, I wanted all the staff on board, keen to hear their views and expectations. It was so encouraging to see the amount of support I had behind me, with every member of staff feeling that this role was well overdue. Much of the nursing team had changed over the past year, so there was also a fair bit of not only getting to know one another, but also looking at how we could complement our working relationships moving forward.

With treatment rumbling along in the background, I was able to plan my working days around facilitating my care at the hospital. My out-of-work time was just as important to my recovery as my in-work time, and it worked so well.

I was surprised at not only how easily I had adjusted to coming back to work after all that had happened, but also to my new role – well, apart from the need to think about what to wear every day rather than just putting a uniform on. It was so lovely to be back amongst people and friends again, especially after spending over a year shielding from them all. So much had happened in my life, and theirs, yet I felt so assured that they would take such good care of me as I continued in my recovery.

With the work needed to develop my post, it was a while before I had any direct patient contact, which fitted in well with Dr Joe's recommendation to avoid people with known respiratory infections for at least 6 months. I sat in on the morning handovers to reorientate myself to this very important time of information-sharing, a time when, if I felt I could contribute, I did.

Clearly, with my newfound ability to relate to certain things such as conditions and treatments, symptoms and interventions, there were times when quite painful memories were triggered, making some days more uncomfortable than others. But I simply took one day at a time, making sure, if needs be, that I talked to someone about how I was feeling. For some staff, being particularly mindful of the potential for this, their asking me first became a very natural and intuitive process, for which I was always so grateful.

Reflecting at the end of each day, I tried hard to blinker myself, working on a need to focus my thoughts on how I could help the patient, family and team, rather than any of it being about me. In time, it got easier and before too long I recognised how much my insights on the journey could bring something completely new to the table.

Having now completed my maintenance treatment, my life was once again free from the ties of treatment days. Some would and did say, 'That's fantastic', but for me – and as I found is the case for many who have also walked this path – the overwhelming feeling of vulnerability was so hard. I really struggled to fully appreciate my newfound freedom. No more regular bloods, checking how I was, giving me something that we knew was keeping the cancer away. I was flying solo after 18 months of adjusting my life. Lynn, as always, knew exactly where I was coming from; she had anticipated my reaction and was there, with her shared understanding, to reassure me of this perfectly normal reaction.

After around 4 months I had started to become increasingly active in post, starting to consider meeting with patients and talking with families/carers. I was particularly mindful that I was still at a greater risk of picking up an infection than before treatment, now that I was back among people again. Covid was still very much at the forefront of people's minds.

The first few times I went and introduced myself to patients were a little nerve-racking. I think because I had been away for what seemed like an age, I had lost some of my confidence, plus I was worried that I might find myself in situations that would push me a little too far. But as I explored and experimented with my new role amongst the team, the reactions and feedback were so encouraging that I knew I could and would make the role work.

The more I met and spoke to patients, the more evident it was how much my own journey through cancer was influencing the conversations we were having. It had brought something completely new to my role, an insight that would allow me to connect on a brand new level. I could understand not only living with a life-limiting condition and all the possible baggage that comes with that, but also the fears and apprehensions of being in a place where you're feeling safe and reassured by the professionals around you, and then having to face a future away from this precious safety blanket.

I was creating some incredibly powerful and valuable professional relationships with those I felt extremely passionate about supporting, as each one remained tethered to the rollercoaster ride that continued to carry them through the various transitions in their journeys. Each meeting was quite different, ranging from being nothing more than an everyday standard meeting to the unspoken impression that, based on what I am saying and clearly understanding, I *might* have been through a similar experience to them, but they didn't always want to ask. Then there was the very direct, 'You're one of us, aren't you?', as the patient made reference to my short and wavy hair. Then there have been times where patients have said how incredibly understanding I have been, and asked if I have had or known someone similar to themselves. When I reveal my experience, I'm told, 'It's just so lovely to speak to someone who really does understand' and 'Thank you for being so honest; people mean well, but don't really understand, do they?'. If just one of these meetings has contributed to helping someone else through yet another time of such uncertainty in their journey, then my decision to return to work has not been in vain.

Life has been good, work has been good and I'm really starting to feel back in control again. We've had a barbeque with family and friends and even managed a family holiday away with Ross, Nic and Grace, just what we all desperately needed. You can't beat time away in beautiful Cornwall; time by the sea, somewhere you can recharge and heal the

body and mind, while, most importantly for me, creating some wonderful memories to hold onto.

Surprising even myself, I also set up a personal challenge; time to give something back. Setting up my fundraiser, I pledged to try and complete a cycle challenge of 100 miles in 30 days and was so happy to have smashed it in only 18 days. So, with the incredible response behind me, I was straight away onto Stage 2, 100 miles, but in just 13 days this time. The weather in Stage 2 was perhaps less considerate, with several rides seeing me return home like a drowned rat, but I did it and I was so proud of myself. Together, we raised an incredible £1,190 for Cancer Research UK, and that had meant the world to me.

# Chapter 16

# It's Back!

It's now January 2022 and my bubble has just burst! I have been ticking along with no problems since my remission in September 2020. I have been feeling great, with no reason at all for concern, having had regular bloods and appointments which have reassured me that all is looking positive. But having just attended another routine follow-up appointment at the hospital, we have been hit with the news that my cancer markers are going up again and they suspect the cancer is back. The cruelty this disease inflicts is unrelenting. There are no words.

I'm going to have another CT scan to see if they can see anything, as they will not plan any further chemotherapy without seeing it on a scan first. Clearly, I'm hoping and praying it's just a ‘blip’ but even so, I have to ask what they will do if it is back. Andy quickly tells me not to think like that, but I am someone who needs to understand and prepare, even if it proves a false alarm. I can just lodge it closer to the back of my mind rather than the front, for now, as I’m assured they will consider rechallenging me with chemo if needs be. The anxiety levels are straight back up again as we go back through the very familiar motions and emotions along with family and friends, who are also certainly not expecting this, again!

With my CT done in less than a week, we’re soon back to clinic and it’s so lovely to be seeing Dr Joe today. He reassures us that there is nothing visible on the latest CT scan, so they will repeat it in six weeks and continue to closely monitor my bloods. He tells us how much he wanted to see me/us today as it’s his last working day before leaving for some time working away in Australia, and wanted to continue to offer his support regardless of where he was in the world, even offering his phone number. Without promising anything, he said he was unsure when he would be back, but that he would be at some point. Whilst clearly very sad that he was going to be leaving, I could only reiterate his words back to him, ‘You must go and live your life too, and I really wish you every happiness'.

Now, in his absence, I have been placed under the care of a new consultant which has left me feeling particularly vulnerable, as she doesn't know me or us from before I started treatment, and she has not been with me throughout my journey to date. I am sure she is lovely, but for me, it's really unsettling to switch consultants, especially at yet another devastating moment in this journey. But I knew Clair had my back and would be there just as much as he would have been. I carried on managing to work, keeping my head busy and trying not to spend too much time thinking of the possible outcomes. Work was a welcome distraction as I tried so hard not to spend too much time worrying about what could possibly be happening inside of me.

Believe me, it wasn't an easy task, especially as I only really switched off when I was in work mode. Subsequently, with work only taking up 6 hours of my day, I had the remaining 18 hours, both day and night, to try and distract my thoughts in some way or another. I could hear Dr Joe saying, 'Go away and live your life', so I decided that we needed to take advantage of a short break away, just in case I was going to be restarting chemo soon. I managed to find us a beautiful hotel at Ambleside in the Lakes, looking out over Lake Windermere and as an extra treat for Andy, I also booked us a VW campervan called 'Rubydoo' to travel up and back in. As with many 'boys and their toys', he was as expected, in his element!

As the next CT appointment looms, so does the only too familiar apprehension as I find myself walking back into the scanning room with my correctly donned designer gowns and socks. I just sense that this is going to be the one that shows up something. So my next worry is, will it be treatable? Thankfully, I don't have to wait too long with Clair on it, and within a matter of days she rings me and asks if I want to be told the results over the phone, or to come and see her. I told her I was sat with Pam at the time, so I asked her to tell me over the phone. As Pam took my hand we both listened intently, and as I had anticipated, it wasn't the news we were desperately wanting to hear.

I had two new small deposits, one on the lining of my liver and another on the lining of the small bowel, and they wanted to restart chemo as soon as possible. When I asked how soon, she came back with Monday: today is Friday. While clearly not looking forward to the prospect of yet more chemo, I actually felt fortunate and grateful to be deemed appropriate to have the chance of more treatment and yes, my head was all over the place, but I'd done it once before and I was determined I would 'crack on' and try and do it all again.

So, yet again I find myself going back through all the motions and emotions, having to let everyone know that we're starting all over again. The one thing I continue to struggle with, more than anything, is just how incredibly hard it is to accept that your journey is causing so much upset and anguish for so many people that you care so much for.

This time round was different again, as I desperately wanted to continue working alongside my treatment if I could. Neil was his usual incredibly supportive self, insisting I put myself first and asking how he could help. Whatever I had decided or would decide, or even if I changed my mind, he would support me 110%, which was just what I needed to hear. With the treatment planned to be the same as previously, I had a good idea of how I might be during treatment. It was going to be a further six cycles, but this time every three weeks and not four. I would have the same post-treatment regime, including the Filgrastim injections for three days to hopefully keep me out of hospital.

Coming back to the CTU after 17 months, it was obvious how much staffing levels had dropped and how the staff were clearly struggling to do what they wanted to do. The strong and admirable team spirit was still clear for all to see, with each staff member doing their best to keep their colleagues going, and the patients were unquestionably right behind them – well, all but one, on my treatment day at least, whose inconsiderate and endless complaining and criticising reflected a belief that they were more entitled to the nurse's time and attention than anyone else. Fortunately, their behaviour was finally and publicly addressed by a nurse who had just about had enough and wasn't prepared to subject staff and patients to any more; her actions were professional, appropriate, warmly welcomed and clearly backed by everyone's very subtle reactions in the department. No wonder too many NHS staff feel so deflated and undervalued.

I chose to balance my time by using the first 7–10 days working remotely and flexibly, banking my hours on the days I felt well enough to work and putting those hours to use when I was less well, or for my treatment days, so as not to accrue sickness hours. After the 7–10 day period, I would then come into work and continue to work my usual hours. I didn't particularly enjoy remote working, as I never felt able to do my job as I wanted to do it, plus the contact with others was so important to me; but it served its purpose and I simply plodded on through the 'delightful' effects of the treatment. Despite feeling apprehensive about coming into work whilst undergoing chemo, I craved being back around people again, so as soon as I felt comfortable coming back, I was back!

Particularly in the hospice, we are always mindful of the nature of our work and how emotionally draining it can be at times, conscious of the possible triggers and signs of stress in colleagues and how to divert or manage any situations as they present. So, for me, with my emotions very much up and down, I also had to be acutely self-aware and ensure, where possible, that I did not put myself into situations which might feel uncomfortably challenging on that day. There would always be the unexpected, so I tried to ensure that I felt strong enough to deal with the chances of that and if I didn't, my colleagues were always ready to step in on my behalf.

Wanting to do my job as fully as possible and simply be effective, I soon grabbed any appropriate opportunity to meet with patients and families again; a time which always brought me back to my hands-on nursing days. This time my journey was certainly more apparent than before, and with full hair loss and my beanie hats brought out of hibernation, the meetings with patients continued along similar lines to before, but this time I was offering an additional qualification, a mutual understanding of recurrence for those in the know.

Patients' reactions, along with their curiosity, would always make me smile; it was almost as if they thought I was a fellow patient wandering in, or perhaps that the hospice had employed a 'token cancer patient' in a supporting role. Once they realised who I was and my role, we would often engage in conversations which many said they had 'not been able to have before, because no one had been able to fully understand'. I listened and engaged, and most of the time it was very comfortable and easy to be having these conversations, but there was the very rare occasion when the dependence felt particularly overwhelming, and I needed to turn to my colleagues to help me deflect the uncomfortable sense of reliance on me, my insight and my time – and they were always there.

My treatment continued for the full six months, as planned, with my cancer markers showing a great response again. So, it was time again to say goodbye to the wonderful safety blanket of the CTU and go back into vulnerable mode. Time for my follow-on CT scan to be arranged and whilst the markers were encouraging, you can never ever relax and assume the scan will tell you what you're hoping for. It was just over two weeks' wait for my scan, so I kept myself busy with work and even managed a short break in Leeds, to use a birthday gift and please don't judge me on this one, but both Andy and myself went to the Emmerdale set for the day. Of course, we had to buy the obligatory *David's Shop* bag and I made sure Andy, perhaps slightly embarrassed, carried it for me. It was a perfectly timed, brilliant day for both of us, and very sunny, so that was my call to don my sunglasses and wide-brimmed hat to protect my pale, bald head, standing out amongst the sun worshippers of the group as we were taken round. But that was absolutely fine.

That day, my hat was nothing more than a sunscreen, and I had two amazing women to thank for that. Both Jane and Jenny were colleagues and more importantly, very dear friends, and what they did for me and so many like me was to raise awareness and support in an incredibly selfless gesture; they were going to 'brave the shave' to fundraise for the hospice and Cancer Research UK, two charities very close to our hearts, for obvious reasons. It was 1st June and a lovely, in fact perfect, sunny day to gather round and offer our support as they quietly and apprehensively chose their seats and took each other's hands, with Chris and Beth on standby to begin the first cuts. I'm still unable to fully explain how emotional it made me feel but I can, to this day, recall those feelings with a smile and genuine flutter in my heart. They looked incredible and actually, even more beautiful, with their facial features now emphasised and an aura of confidence and pride that was radiating from within.

It was now my time to make a very public speech, not only in recognition of what they had done, but to give a little insight into life with enforced hair loss – that feeling of looking in the mirror and not recognising the person in the reflection anymore, where your very private journey soon becomes very public, for the world to see. I would never have thought that I could speak so openly and publicly about such an emotional part of my life, but the importance of the message I wanted to get across far outweighed any apprehension I was feeling. Because of these incredible women, this day was the last day I wore my beanie hat and it felt so liberating.

It did cross my mind what the patients and visitors might think, seeing all three of us with very little hair, but in fact it ended up being a great conversation starter for many. Sitting down with one patient, she asked me if I was another one of the girls who'd had her head shaved for their colleague, and when I explained that I was 'the colleague', she simply took my hand as we looked into each other's eyes, with a sense of mutual understanding, and simply smiled. Her perhaps embarrassed but unnecessary need to apologise was soon quashed and after a few naturally inquisitive questions about me, I steered the conversation back to her, as we sat and explored her thoughts and fears for the future.

# Chapter 17

# Living with Uncertainty

Well, it's now been three weeks since my latest scan and we're finally heading back to the hospital for my results. The same sense of dread encompasses both our thoughts and emotions as, once again, we take the short journey to the hospital, barely speaking a word, almost fearful of voicing our hope out loud. As we walk through the Outpatients department, I'm looking around and thinking of the reasons why everyone else is here; are their lives in turmoil too, or is life good and their visit no more than an overhaul? Bang on time, we're invited into the consulting room where we tentatively take our seats, waiting patiently, wanting but at the same time not wanting her to say what's on the scan images. 'Julia, there is no evidence of disease on your scan and your markers are wonderful'.

It was amazing news, yet my emotions felt somehow suppressed and more reserved this time. To me, it felt like *Yes, I've done it again*, but then also thinking, *I've been here before and no doubt I will be here again*. There was no urge today to want to go out and say 'Excuse me, can I tell you I've just been told today that I've beaten cancer?'. I'm certainly not a pessimist, but in this moment I couldn't suppress those thoughts that were niggling away inside. I never shared those thoughts out loud; I didn't want everyone to have to consider the possibility too, so instead I simply allowed them, rightly, to embrace their moment.

The team had already discussed and planned for me to start a new maintenance treatment, this time in the form of twice daily tablets and whilst I must still attend CTU every four weeks for reviews, life can otherwise carry on relatively normally. Apparently, it's a relatively new treatment and one that has shown some very encouraging results, which is promising, but as with most medications, they will come with a 'delightful' list of potential side effects to watch out for. So, we can only keep our fingers crossed that they do the job and hope that they are kind to me.

Life has managed to be almost 'normal' again. After a month of taking the new tablets, I don't want to say too much in case I jinx myself, but I think I am getting away quite lightly, so far anyway. With yet another hurdle behind me, it's full steam ahead as we prepare for our holiday down in Cornwall with Pam and Mick and I couldn't wish to for anything more right now. My decision to go has been in the balance for far too long, clouded by the uncertainty of this punishing journey; but regardless of what the scan might have shown and the possible side effects I might or might not have experienced, I needed this time, we all desperately needed this time.

We really couldn't have wished for a better place to be, such a beautiful part of the country, somewhere that allowed each of us, all the space and time we needed to start and heal some very personal wounds. The days ahead created many opportunities for some gentle reflection, both quietly alone and together. We embraced the familiar sites along with the wonderful memories they provoked, allowing us to relive some very special family times in this beautiful and exceptional part of the country. We also enjoyed plenty of fun and laughter, created precious memories and simply embraced our incredibly special friendship together.

One particular day was a day that will remain with me always; it was when Pam and I got the chance to swim with horses. It was my gift to her, something to treasure and look back on with such fondness. To be able to ride bareback from the stables down to the seashores and be graced by the beautiful backdrop of St Michaels Mount, was an incredible experience. Then, with our wetsuits on, we tentatively walked into the, shall we say, 'tad cold' waters that awaited us and prepared to remount our four-legged friends. All I can say is, once THAT embarrassing moment was out of the way, it was truly incredible and would highly recommend it as an addition to any bucket list.

For some, there are times and places in your life where the not so good memories that you've tried to suppress for so long become too much to carry. I'm unsure if it was the fact that I was somewhere that provoked certain childhood memories, or perhaps my journey, or both, that lead me to think more deeply about those who had always been in my life yet had failed me and the rest of our family so badly in those younger years. But it soon transpired that this was apparently 'my time and my place' and by having Pam there, in that moment, I'd found a new inner strength, one that would release me from a haunting past and guide me through a pathway that offered some degree of closure.

Whilst the days we shared seemed to pass so quickly, the memories and time we created for ourselves reminded us of just how precious life can be and how important it is to live your best life. We are all surrounded by people who influence our lives in some way or another, some good and others not so good and it's often not until those people have gone from our lives that we realise the impact they have had on us.

On Thursday 8th of September, just the start of our holiday, we had been having a few drinks at the local pub, talking over our plans for the week ahead and sharing our fond stories of our experiences of Cornwall. As my phone sat on the table, a 'breaking news' alert caught my eye as it came up on the main screen. The royal family were said to be travelling to be at the bedside of Queen Elizabeth II, in what was soon to become apparent were her last hours of life. In effect, we, along with the rest of the world, had just been served notice to prepare for the loss of the Queen, the longest-reigning British monarch and the world's longest-reigning female monarch in history. As we returned to the cottage to sit together and watch the news as it continued to unfold, it felt like an unbelievably emotional and reflective moment in history, when the world had suddenly become united in grief.

The days that followed left me with mixed emotions. I felt so much for the royal family, however, it was not entirely for their loss, but instead for their extremely public journey through such raw grief. As I too had experienced a very public journey through grief, albeit in a completely different context and on a considerably reduced scale, I couldn't help but feel distracted by my understanding of how hard that must have been for them through the days that followed.

With our wonderful holiday having come to a close and a less enjoyable nine-hour return journey behind us, we were finally back home and desperate to pick up Trigger from his own 'little doggy holiday' with Josie and Nigel. We had missed each other so much and that was never more apparent as 'Trigg' constantly flitted between us, in search of our unwavering attention. It's funny, isn't it, despite how much you enjoy a holiday, there really is nowhere quite like home.

So, with the pasties safely delivered to family and all the post-holiday jobs out of the way, I was soon preparing myself to step back into work mode yet again. For me, work has never just been a place to go and get paid for what I do, it's a place where I can live 'my' life, make a difference, connect, heal and share invaluable knowledge. When people have asked if I've stopped working, I think to myself, 'Why would I, whilst I am so fortunate to feel well enough to do so?'. Work has always been a big part of my life, nurtured by the same goals and aspirations I've always had, so I simply smile and let them know I am.

As the months passed and my regular check-ups with oncology continued, I'd had no reason for concern, or so I'd thought. That was until I found myself sitting in the consulting room having been hit with the ever familiar news that my cancer markers had begun to climb once again. Despite a repeat CT scan showing no signs of spread, the markers continued to climb over the coming months and I began to psychologically prepare myself for what was to come next. Would treatment be offered, or would this not be an option this time? A second scan three months later identified two areas with small deposits and ultimately resulted in me facing my third round of treatment.

Feeling a little reflective over the days that followed, I found myself looking through my collection of photographs on my phone, something that provoked a multitude of feelings. One thing that really struck me was, despite what I had felt to be the illness taking away my freedom to live my best life, I had actually very much lived my life, albeit very differently to what I had once envisaged, but that was somehow OK. It reminded me that I hadn't allowed myself to simply sit back and let this 'thing' dominate my life; I had, however, been fortunate and therefore able to dig deep in order to try and make space for it, adjusting to 'surviving' in its unrelenting wake.

The photographs proved a valuable reminder of all the moments, some perhaps painful ones, but mostly very happy and fulfilled times, where the much-loved people in my life have walked and continue to walk right beside me, enabling me to remain strong, focused and, above all else, still me. The unrelenting support has been such a humbling experience, by no means limited in any way to family and close friends. With the additional support of colleagues, professionals, neighbours, good friends and even strangers, all offering their unrelenting love, support and prayers, I remain forever grateful for having them in my life. It can sometimes be the random acts of kindness or perhaps the smallest of gestures, that the giver might feel to be less than adequate, but to the person in receipt of your thoughtfulness, it means so much and is never forgotten.

Having the opportunity to bring my story to so many has left me feeling exceptionally privileged and proud. I look back and realise just how far I have come, yet still know deep down that the rollercoaster journey ahead will be just as tough as the tracks I've already travelled. Every appointment, blood test and scan will continue to be clouded by some very painful memories and will remain just as difficult as the last. Every twinge will be a cruel reminder of possibility and the hesitancy to make plans for too far ahead, will probably never leave us. But I can and will continue to dig deep for as long as I am able, and aim to live my best life, in the shadows of unrelenting uncertainty.

Nothing has changed, I'm still the same person you have had the chance to get to know, focused, strong and just happy to continue embracing life, photographing the priceless memories and finding laughter despite the darkness. I hope to carry on as I have previously, of course led by my response to the new treatment, and simply continue to take one precious day at a time.

I hope my 'journey on the other side' has provided a safe place for you to explore some of your own thoughts and fears, curiosities and interests, perhaps allayed fears of being alone and even offered some clarity and guidance for the tomorrows. No one knows what tomorrow will bring, so don't wait for it to come, don't wait for things to get better, just embrace the here and now.

# Acknowledgements

I never could have imagined I would find myself writing a book, let alone a book that shared so much of my life with so many. So without a doubt, my first thanks must go to the wonderful Des McCabe, my fellow writer, coach and a leading expert on inclusion and personal development, whose genuine interest, encouragement and belief in me inspired me to put pen to paper once again.

Thank you to all the incredible NHS staff at both Stafford County and UHNM, Dr Joe and Clair Turner, for your unrelenting commitment, dedication and service, which have seen me through some of my darkest of days.

To my wonderful family and dear friends who have walked this journey beside me every day.

As for my incredible network of friends and colleagues who have shown so much love and support, for which I will be forever grateful, I simply cannot write any specific names, as you have all supported me in your own wonderful ways with such kind, sincere and reassuring words, gestures, cuddles, gifts, songs and by just being you.

For my strong, determined and beautiful friends and loved ones, Aunty Pam, 'sister' Pam, Lynn, Kim, Alison, Rachel and Kathryn who have all challenged such adversity, yet still managed to keep pushing forward and embracing laughter, despite the darkness. You were, and are, such incredible and inspirational people and I am so grateful to have had you in my life.

Printed in Great Britain
by Amazon

21220923R00120